HOME
INSULATION

HOME INSULATION

Julian Worthington
and David Knight

W. Foulsham & Co. Ltd.

London · New York · Toronto · Cape Town · Sydney

W. Foulsham & Company Limited
Yeovil Road, Slough, Berkshire, SL1 4JH

ISBN 0-572-01293-4

Photoset in Great Britain by C. R. Barber & Partners
(Highlands) Ltd., Fort William, Scotland, and
printed in Hong Kong.

We should like to thank the following for their help
and co-operation in producing this book:

British Gypsum, DIY Plastics Ltd, Douglas Kane
Ltd, Everest Double Glazing Ltd, Fibreglass Ltd,
Gledhill (Water Storage) Ltd, Hall & Co Ltd of
Maidstone, Homewarm Ltd, Lumite Ltd, Shell
Thermocomfort Ltd. Particular thanks are due to
Duraflex Products Ltd for supplying aluminium
sliding and plastic hinged double glazing systems.

Photographs: British Gypsum – 54, 55, 57; Douglas
Kane Ltd – 32, 59; Everest Double Glazing Ltd –
20, 102; Fibreglass Ltd – 30, 31, 43, 62; Gledhill
(Water Storage) Ltd – 18 (right); Homewarm Ltd –
41; Lumite Ltd – 74; Shell Thermocomfort Ltd – 42.

Cover photograph: British Gypsum.

Contents

Introduction

No-one needs to be reminded of the cost of home heating, whatever the fuel used. Of the total energy costs – electricity, gas, oil and solid fuel – in the average home, up to 80% is spent on providing heating and hot water.

The most depressing fact is that all the heat generated in the home is eventually lost, and the quicker the heat is lost, the more energy you will need to provide more heat to maintain a comfortable living environment. Fortunately the reverse also applies, so that the slower the heat is lost the lower your energy requirements and therefore the lower the fuel bill will be.

The aim of this book is to explain what you can do to slow down the heat loss by providing adequate insulation in those areas of the home that offer the most effective escape routes for heat.

Of course insulation is not the complete or only answer to wasted energy, which can equally result from poor housekeeping or extravagant use of hot water. In these circumstances you can effect considerable savings by giving more thought to the use of energy in the home and by taking appropriate action.

Energy savings

From a hygiene point of view it is good practice to give all the rooms in the home a regular 'airing', particularly in bedrooms and bathroom, where windows may not normally be opened so frequently. When you throw open the windows to let in the fresh air, however, remember to switch off any heating since there is little point in wasting money warming the air from outside.

Where central heating has been installed in a house, there is no value in wasting heat in rooms that are not being used. Turn off the radiators in all unused areas and make sure that where you are keeping the heat going, all doors out of those rooms are kept shut.

If you are out at work all day, make sure you switch off the heating. The value of a time control on the boiler is that it can be adjusted to switch on the heating to warm the house by the time you arrive back. For the amount it will save in fuel costs, this small investment is well worth while.

Check the temperature settings around the house, since the chances are that they are too high. The normal recommendation on temperature levels in living rooms is 21°C and for other areas in the home 18°C.

The requirements will obviously vary from household to household. Elderly people who spend much of their time sitting indoors may need a slightly higher temperature. They can remain comfortable in slightly lower temperatures by wearing thicker clothing. You will be surprised what a difference you can achieve in fuel costs by turning down a room thermostat by just a few degrees.

The bathroom is the greatest area of waste for hot water. When you consider that with every bath you take you are probably using in the region of 20 gallons of hot water, which is then thrown away, the fitting of a shower over the bath – or installing a separate shower cubicle – becomes a sensible investment. A five minute shower will use up 5–10 gallons of hot water, so already you are cutting your hot water costs in half.

One added advantage with a shower is that you and others will probably be able to get into the bathroom that much quicker during peak periods of demand.

Check the temperature of your hot water, since the chances are it is running hotter than it need do for most requirements. A temperature of around 60°C is usually quite adequate for the average needs. If you do run it much hotter than this, you will only waste the heat by topping it up with cold water anyway. Even a small adjustment to the boiler's thermostat will save you money.

The value of insulation

The object of insulation in the home is to increase the resistance to heat flow through walls, ceilings, roofs, floors, windows and doors, thus slowing down the rate at which heat is lost to the surroundings.

It is, of course, impossible to prevent the eventual loss of heat from the home. But the longer it takes for the heat to escape, the more the heat is retained indoors. Not only does this add to the comfort of your home, but it also cuts down on the amount of energy needed to maintain a constant temperature.

Imagine you are sitting in a tent on a frosty night, when you will need a great deal of heat inside to keep you warm. This would have to be continuous, since the heat would rapidly be lost to the atmosphere. By moving into the garden shed, you could reduce the amount of heat required since the walls would retain it longer than canvas.

The principle of insulation to retain heat is well demonstrated in a thermos flask. To measure its effect, put a pint of boiling water into a milk bottle and another into a thermos flask. The water in the bottle will be cold in about 45 minutes, while that in the flask will still be very hot four or five hours later. This is because the walls of the flask have excellent insulation properties that resist the flow of heat, while the glass bottle has virtually none.

The right type of insulation in the appropriate places will reduce your energy bill. But it is important to bear in mind the cost-effectiveness of the different forms of insulation and work out what best suits your situation and requirements.

The cost-effectiveness of insulation

It is possible to spend thousands of pounds on insulating your home and thus reduce the amount of heat lost dramatically. As a result, you would see a large percentage reduction in the heating costs. But the savings you might make would be unlikely to exceed £150–200 each year and on that basis it would take many years to recover the cost of installing complete insulation.

Although improvements of this kind are to an extent reflected in an increase of value to the property, it will not be that considerable. Should you decide to move after only a few years, you would certainly be out of pocket.

If you intend to remain in your present house for a reasonable length of time, then the value of more thorough insulation increases. Otherwise you should concentrate on those types of insulation that offer a good return for the money you have available to spend over a shorter period.

It is, of course, impossible to be precise in your calculations, since you cannot predict the exact amount you will save on energy and equally you cannot guarantee fuel prices. On the other hand, you can safely assume that fuel will only get more expensive. This in turn will improve the cost-effectiveness of any insulation you install now. As the savings increase, so the 'pay-back' period will be reduced.

This book offers some guidance to the approximate savings in heat loss – and therefore energy costs – to be gained from the various types of insulation and from this you should be able to work out reasonably accurately the cost-effectiveness of each one. Here is a summary of the main areas to be considered in the most likely order of merit against cost and savings.

1. Hot water cylinder jacket By fitting a jacket to the hot water cylinder you could well recover its cost in a matter of weeks.

2. Loft insulation Depending on the age of your house, some form of insulation may already be installed in the loft (see pages 23–30). If you have to insulate that area from scratch, the likely pay-back period for the average house will be one to two years.

3. Draughtproofing The heat you can lose due to draughts is surprisingly high (see pages 78–100). The cost of this work throughout the home is not likely to be very high and could well be recovered within the first heating season.

4. Cavity wall insulation This is not a DIY job and will have to be done by a contractor. The different processes available (see pages 39–43) are all very efficient and therefore cost-effective. The pay-back period will depend on the construction of your house and could be anything from three to seven years.

5. Double glazing The savings in heat loss from installing double glazing will depend on the type and size of your windows. Less advantage is gained from double-glazing small windows – more for large windows. In terms of heat loss reduction alone, the pay-back period is difficult to define and will of course depend on the type of double glazing that is installed (see pages 101–116). Certainly with professionally installed systems, you should be looking to at least a 10-year investment. You should, however, bear in mind that double glazing does offer other benefits, such as sound insulation and security, which are difficult to cost and particularly the greater comfort within the room, since by insulating the windows this way you slow down the rate at which air circulates and eliminate cold down draughts from the windows. This enables you to use all the floor space in comfort, even on the coldest day. Despite the fact that this is one of the primary reasons for installing double glazing, because it is difficult to cost

no account is taken of this benefit when calculating investment costs and pay-back periods.

6. Other types of insulation Depending on the age and construction of your house, you may find other types of insulation are cost-effective. These would include internal and external wall insulation, as well as floor and ceiling insulation. The cost-effectiveness here would have to be estimated according to individual circumstances.

Guidance when buying

Having decided on the type of insulation you want to have installed in your home, you may opt to get the work done professionally. To help you in your choice of the best product at the right price, here are some general points to bear in mind before you make a purchase.

From the advice given here, the inference should not necessarily be to mistrust every salesman who knocks on your door. But you would be well advised to forearm yourself, just in case.

1. Remember that you will in many cases be dealing with highly trained salesmen who have been taught to sell their product against all opposition. They will use a whole range of inducements to get you to buy their product rather than any other.

2. Never be afraid or feel it impolite to say no or to ask for time to consider the quotation. You must never be rushed into making a decision you may later regret.

3. Avoid getting a salesman to call late in the evening. He may keep you talking for hours and will probably wear you down in the process.

4. Some salesmen may claim to be carrying out market research and say that they are not interested in selling anything. Be on your guard and ask for some means of identification that they are bona-fide researchers.

5. Always ask for proof that the company they work for is a member of a relevant trade association.

6. Always get three or four written quotations for the same job so that you can make an accurate comparison between prices. And never tell the last salesman who quotes that he is the last, otherwise he will try to make the sale there and then.

7. Remember that no-one can give an accurate quotation without first measuring your property.

8. Ask the salesman why he considers his product is better than anyone else's and never be persuaded just because his prices are cheaper.

9. You may be offered a special discount if you make a decision at the salesman's first call. You must resist this temptation. It will probably apply anyway should you decide to buy that product and you then have a good bargaining basis for ensuring you get any discount available.

10. It is quite likely that you will be told prices are going up very shortly or that you are being offered a 'special deal', if you accept immediately. It is usually just sales talk and you should not be taken in by this.

11. You may well be offered special financial arrangements for paying. Before you commit yourself, compare the deal you have been offered with similar loans from your bank or building society.

12. The salesman may also try to interest you in associated products or services. Again you must make sure that you need them and that you can afford them before having them written into a quotation.

13. You must insist that the different quotations you are getting are put in writing and then compare them on your own before reaching a decision.

14. When you finally decide to place an order, make absolutely sure that a completion date is written into the final contract – and, of course, give yourself plenty of time to read EVERY WORD of the contract carefully before signing. If in doubt get it checked. Never take the salesman's word for it.

15. Remember that even after you have signed the contract, provided that the company is a member of an official trade association and that you sign in your home, you should still be able to cancel your order within a few days without losing your deposit.

Grants for home insulation

Since much emphasis has been put on energy conservation and the economic use of existing resources, local authorities have been empowered to give grants to help towards the cost of certain forms of insulation in the home. At present these are available for part of the cost of installing loft insulation where it does not exist. They also cover the insulation of pipes in the loft and hot water cylinders and installing an access flap into the loft if none exists.

If you feel you might qualify for a grant, you should contact your local authority before starting work. It may wish to check on the job before it offers any money and will, in any case, tell you which materials may be used and the minimum thickness of the insulation. Special consideration may be given to elderly people or those severely disabled applicants who are on a low income.

The grant scheme is available in situations where no insulation at present exists and also where there is 30 mm ($1\frac{1}{2}$ in) or less thickness of loft insulation. So check with your local authority if you have this situation in your loft in case you are eligible for a grant.

1 Heat loss in the home

All the energy used to heat the home is eventually lost; it is impossible to retain it indefinitely. The object of the book is to show you how you can delay the loss of heat as long as possible to gain the maximum benefit for the lowest cost. Depending on your budget, you must decide what savings you are prepared to make according to the different areas of the home that need to be insulated.

We have taken as a typical example a semi-detached house built in the 1950s and have indicated where heat losses mainly occur and by how much they can be reduced (see diagram on page 12).

Legislation is continually being introduced and upgraded to maintain minimum acceptable standards of insulation in newly built homes. The principle aims are to conserve energy on a national basis and at the same time save you money by saving your heat. You do not need reminding that with the ever-increasing cost of fuel, insulation is becoming more and more cost-effective, particularly in older properties where it is either inadequate or does not exist. Just to emphasise the importance of insulation, grants are available to assist with the installation.

Before discussing the different means by which you can insulate your home and save on fuel costs, it is important that you understand the principles involved in heat loss and how they are measured. This will help you to work out how much insulation you will need and how effective it will be.

Heat loss values

These are listed as k, R and U values, which are used to measure the heat loss through a material.

Thermal conductivity (k value) This is the measurement of the ability of a material to conduct heat and it is measured through one metre of the material. The unit used for this value is watts per metre degree C (w/m°C).

Thermal resistance (R value) This is the measurement for the resistance to heat flow of a material in relation to its thickness. It is obtained by dividing the thickness (in metres) by the k value of the material. The higher the R value, the better the resistance to heat flow. The unit for this value is square metre degree C per watts (m²°C/w).

Thermal transmittance (U value) This is the rate of heat flow through a unit area of a structure when a temperature difference exists between the air on each side of the structure. The unit for this value is watts per square metre degree C (w/m²°C). The value is calculated by taking the reciprocal of the sum of the thermal resistances (R values) of the component parts of the structure, plus the thermal resistances of the surfaces and any cavity within the structure. Thus U = 1/total R. With U values, the lower the value, the better the insulation factor.

To help you compare different materials, the following tables of k, R and U values have been included. Bear in mind, however, that the figures are only approximate, since there are variations between products from different manufacturers and grades of materials.

k values

Material	w/m°C
Brick	0.8
Glass	1.05
Hardboard	0.094
Plasterboard	0.159
Plywood	0.138
Timber (pine)	0.138
Rendering	0.55

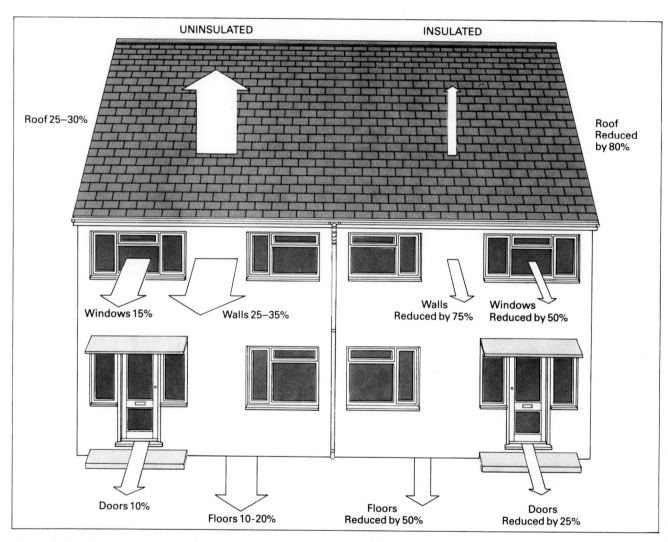

UNINSULATED

INSULATED

Roof 25–30%

Roof Reduced by 80%

Windows 15%

Walls 25–35%

Walls Reduced by 75%

Windows Reduced by 50%

Doors 10%

Floors 10-20%

Floors Reduced by 50%

Doors Reduced by 25%

With this pair of semi-detached houses, the one on the left has no insulation fitted and the percentage heat losses through the roof, walls, windows, doors and floors are shown. The house on the right has been fully insulated and here the percentage reduction in heat losses is shown. The figures are, of course, based on the average efficiency of the various insulation methods mentioned in this book.

R values

Material	$m^2{}^\circ C/w$
102 mm brick (exposed)	0.122
12 mm lightweight plaster	0.075
2 mm sarking felt	0.01
3 layers of 2 mm roofing felt	0.037
10 mm plywood	0.071
25 mm softwood	0.192
100 mm concrete	0.071
25 mm thermal board	0.42
50 mm thermal board	1.08

Surface resistances:

Wall – external	0.055
Wall – internal	0.123
Roof – external	0.045
Roof – internal	0.106

U values

(depending on how exposed the property is to weather conditions)

Material	$w/m^2{}^\circ C$
225 mm (or 9 in) solid brickwork	2.17
Brick cavity wall – 50 mm (2 in) cavity/breeze block	1.37
Brick cavity wall – 50 mm (2 in) cavity/concrete block	0.96
Brick cavity wall – 50 mm (2 in) cavity/100 mm (4 in) insulating block/13 mm ($\frac{1}{2}$ in) plaster	0.89
Brick cavity wall – 50 mm (2 in) insulated cavity/100 mm (4 in) insulating block/12 mm ($\frac{1}{2}$ in) plaster	0.43
Flat roof – 3 layers felt/chipboard/joists/plasterboard	1.05
Flat roof – 3 layers felt/chipboard/no joists/plasterboard	1.59
Flat roof – 16 mm ($\frac{5}{8}$ in) plaster/150 mm (6 in) concrete/vapour barrier/50 mm (2 in) roof board/7 mm ($\frac{1}{4}$ in) felt/10 mm ($\frac{3}{8}$ in) chippings	0.54
Typical domestic 30° pitched roof/tiles on sarking felt/no loft insulation	2.5
Typical domestic 30° pitched roof/tiles on sarking felt/25 mm (1 in) insulation	0.9
Typical domestic 30° pitched roof/tiles on sarking felt/50 mm (2 in) insulation	0.55
Typical domestic 30° pitched roof/tiles on sarking felt/75 mm (3 in) insulation	0.39
Typical domestic 30° pitched roof/tiles on sarking felt/100 mm (4 in) insulation	0.33
Single glazed skylight	6.8
Wooden floor/ventilated/on joists/air bricks on one side of house only/bare surface	0.61
Wooden floor/ventilated/on joists/air bricks on one side of house only/covered with linoleum, vinyl or parquet	0.59
Wooden floor/ventilated/on joists/air bricks on more than one side of house/bare or covered surface	0.82/0.69
Solid floor in contact with earth	0.56
Intermediate wooden floors/on joists/plasterboard ceiling/heat passing upwards	1.7
Intermediate wooden floors/on joists/plasterboard ceiling/heat passing downwards	1.5

U values for glazing

Material	$w/m^2{}^\circ C$
Single glazing	5.6
Double glazing – 6 mm ($\frac{1}{4}$ in) gap	3.4
Double glazing – 9 mm ($\frac{3}{8}$ in) gap	3.2
Double glazing – 12 mm ($\frac{1}{2}$ in) gap	3.0
Double glazing – 20 mm ($\frac{3}{4}$ in) gap	2.9

With windows, however, a new concept called 'effective U value' is used. This takes into account the actual heat gains that can take place in winter, due to the direction in which the windows face and the action of the sun.

Effective U value for single glazing

Material	$w/m^2{}^\circ C$
North-facing window	4.36
East/west-facing window	3.62
South-facing window	2.27

Effective U value for double glazing ($12 \text{ mm}/\frac{1}{2}$ in gap)

Materials	$w/m^2{}^\circ C$
North-facing window	1.92
East/west-facing window	1.28
South-facing window	0.10

Using these figures, you can see that a large double-glazed south-facing window can be of great benefit to a house, having a better insulation value than a wall.

Calculating heat loss

By taking the relevant U values into your calculation, you can work out the heat loss for each room or area in the house. But your calculation will only be of proper value if you take every surface in the room into account – and this means all four walls, windows, doors, ceiling and floor. The best way to calculate the heat loss – working in metres – is as follows:

1. Measure the area of all the walls (height × length) in the room. Keep separate the figures for external and internal walls.
2. Measure the area of all the windows in the room.
3. Measure the area of the floor in the room.
4. Measure the area of the ceiling in the room.
5. List the U values for each of the above areas you have measured.

Next you will need to calculate the temperature differences either side of each surface for the areas you have just measured. When estimating the internal temperature of living rooms, you can work on an average of 21°C. For bedrooms, hallways and landings in a centrally heated house work on 18°C. With any rooms normally unheated, you will need an accurate temperature reading and these rooms should be measured individually. When working out external temperatures, it is best to take the average winter day-time level of −1°C.

To arrive at the heat loss in watts for each room, take the surface areas and multiply them by the relevant U values and the difference in temperature between the inside and outside of each surface. By adding up these totals you will get the total heat loss for that room. Then repeat the calculation taking into account the reduced U values when specific areas have been insulated with the relevant material. You can then check on the savings you would be making in heat loss, depending on the course of action you decide to take.

Cost-efficiency of insulation

By spending literally thousands of pounds on all the various types of insulation you can drastically reduce the amount of heat loss in your home. Taking into account the savings in the cost of fuel, however, this sort of outlay would take many years to recover. On the other hand, you will continue to lose a large amount in wasted fuel each year if you take no steps to insulate at least part of your home.

The ideal solution for most homes, therefore, is a compromise, balancing the cost of certain types of insulation against an increased amount of heat saved.

One of the main factors affecting your decision to increase the insulation is how long you intend to remain in that particular property. Of course you cannot move the insulation with you when you leave and the increased value of your house through carrying out this type of improvement will not

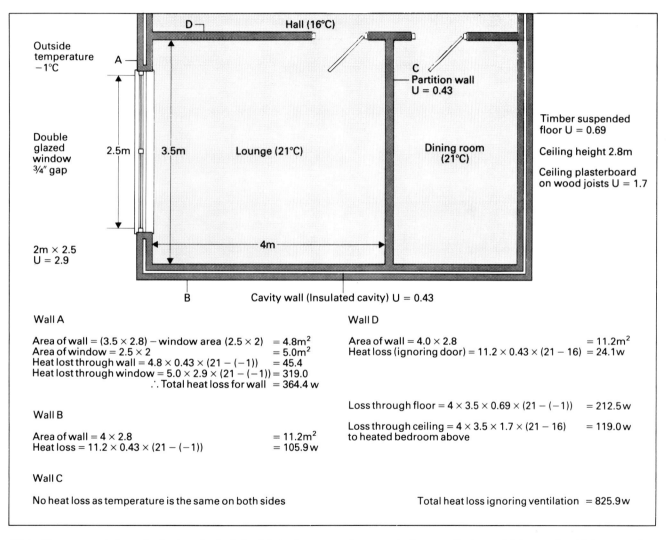

Wall A

Area of wall = (3.5 × 2.8) − window area (2.5 × 2)	= 4.8m²
Area of window = 2.5 × 2	= 5.0m²
Heat lost through wall = 4.8 × 0.43 × (21 − (−1))	= 45.4
Heat lost through window = 5.0 × 2.9 × (21 − (−1))	= 319.0
∴ Total heat loss for wall	= 364.4 w

Wall B

Area of wall = 4 × 2.8	= 11.2m²
Heat loss = 11.2 × 0.43 × (21 − (−1))	= 105.9 w

Wall C

No heat loss as temperature is the same on both sides

Wall D

Area of wall = 4.0 × 2.8	= 11.2m²
Heat loss (ignoring door) = 11.2 × 0.43 × (21 − 16)	= 24.1w

Loss through floor = 4 × 3.5 × 0.69 × (21 − (−1))	= 212.5w
Loss through ceiling = 4 × 3.5 × 1.7 × (21 − 16) to heated bedroom above	= 119.0 w

Total heat loss ignoring ventilation = 825.9w

This diagram and the calculations included with it show how heat loss can be estimated in a room. Here we have taken a typical living room as an example. You will note that to simplify the calculations, no allowance has been made for ventilation, which you should in normal cases take into account. When making your calculations, include all surfaces in the room, working out windows and doors separately for the exterior and interior walls.

15

normally be as high as the cost of carrying out the insulation work.

If, for example, you only intend to spend another two or three years in your present home, then you will be unwise to invest in costly insulation that you will not personally benefit from financially in the relatively short time you plan to remain there. Should you, however, be well settled in your home and have no immediate plans for moving, then it is worth considering a longer-term investment. This is particularly relevant if you are approaching retirement, when you will probably not have so much money to spend on those ever-increasing fuel bills.

You must take into account these and other relevant factors, with the help of the information in this book, before you commit yourself to any cost-intensive installation work. One fact that will not alter, however, is the continual rise in the price of fuel. So any investment now is bound to pay dividends in the long term.

The time it will take to pay back the capital outlay on any particular type of insulation will vary depending on the type of property and how it is run. So it is impossible to be specific about the cost-effectiveness of different kinds of insulation. Such factors as the situation of the house (whether exposed or sheltered), the type of dwelling (detached, semi-detached, bungalow, etc), the amount of central heating (full, partial or none) and the number of people living in the home all play a part in any accurate calculations.

As a guide, however, the following type of property is likely to be the most expensive to heat and therefore the most likely to benefit from additional insulation: an exposed detached bungalow built during or before the 1950s with full central heating and four or more people living there. In contrast, a modern, sheltered, terraced house with partial central heating and two people living in it will be much cheaper to heat and the cost-effectiveness of

extra insulation would in this situation need to be worked out much more carefully.

The Department of Energy has investigated the costs and likely pay-back period for various types of insulation in conjunction with different types of heating in its booklet *A Guide to Home Heating Costs*. The following table will provide a guide to the average pay-back periods for different types of insulation if installed by a contractor. These will be less if you do the jobs yourself. Costs will, of course, vary and it must be stressed that these figures are only an average:

Insulation	Pay-back period
Hot water cylinder jacket	6–8 weeks
Draughtproofing	1 year
Loft insulation	2 years
Cavity wall insulation	3–7 years
Double glazing	6–15 years

The length of time it will take to recover your investment in reduced fuel bills will obviously depend on the extent of the insulation in each category, but these figures are based on doing a complete job on an average semi-detached house taking the average price charged by a recognised contractor.

To give you a reminder of where and how heat loss can be reduced around the home, the following table will provide a useful guide when deciding how to spend your money most effectively:

Structure	Insulation	Reduction in heat flow
Cavity walls	Foam fibre or bead	75%
Windows	Double glazing	50%
	Double glazing with low emissivity glass or triple glazing	75%
Lofts	100 mm (4 in) mineral or cellulose fibre	80%

Structure	Insulation	Reduction in heat flow
Suspended floors	50 mm (2 in) polystyrene	80%
Solid floors	25 mm (1 in) floor insulation	50%

Estimating the savings

Before you can work out roughly how much you can save from the various types of insulation, you will need to estimate how much you spend each year on just heating your home. With those fuels that are used only for heating – such as solid fuel, oil or off-peak electricity – you can do this simply by adding up the relevant bills for each quarter or period over the last 12 months.

The calculation for gas or normal electricity is not quite so straightforward, since these fuels are not used solely for heating, but also to supply general power for other appliances around the home. To get a rough, but reasonably accurate estimate of the cost of heating alone, deduct the total amount of the units used from the period of May to September from those used during October to April, since it is during the latter period that you mainly heat the home. This will, of course, depend on your location.

Having estimated this amount as the total loss, you can then apportion the way it is lost by referring to the heat loss diagram (see page 15). To determine how cost-effective each type of insulation is likely to be, take the total cost of heating the home and from that work out the percentage of the cost in terms of heat loss for each part of the home.

Taking the example of a typical semi-detached house, the following would be average savings:

Heating costs (winter costs less summer costs) = £300
Heat loss through uninsulated cavity walls (25% of total costs) = £75

Heat lost through windows (15% of total cost) = £45

Having worked out the cost of the heat loss, now calculate the savings likely from adding extra insulation:

Saving of heat loss due to cavity wall insulation = 75% of £75 = £56.25
Saving of heat loss due to double glazing = 50% of £45 = £22.50

Now work out the cost of having the installation work carried out by a contractor:

Cavity wall insulation = £350
Double glazing = £1000–£3000*

(*You can probably install a DIY system for around £800)

On the basis that fuel prices remain the same, you can see from these figures that it will take 5–6 years for you to recover the outlay on cavity wall insulation. With double glazing, however, there is much more to take into account than just the insulation factor. The added comfort you gain from being able to use more of the room, the benefit of added security, the prevention of all external window draughts and the saving in external decoration and maintenance costs must also be considered in the overall savings from installing double glazing.

Bear in mind that these figures are only approximate and will vary from house to house. But they do serve as an example of the type of saving that can be made and how long it will take you to recoup the cost of installation.

You will see from the above calculations that it is not easy to get accurate figures. But you should also bear in mind that there are other benefits besides the purely financial ones. For example, the fitting of double glazing and cavity wall insulation will add considerably to the overall comfort in the home throughout the year. Another advantage of fitting replacement aluminium-framed windows is that you

Insulation jackets can be bought to fit all sizes of hot water cylinders. You must ensure when fitting one of these that there are no gaps between the panels and you do not bind them so tight that the insulation is pinched.

If you are installing a new hot water cylinder, it is a good idea to fit one that is already insulated. This type of cylinder has a jacket of polyurethane foam already built in around it and no further insulation is needed.

automatically cut down decoration costs and this type of frame should survive external conditions that much longer.

Getting priorities right

Naturally what you insulate first and how far you take the insulation will depend on circumstances, as previously discussed. But when planning insulation in the average house, the order of priority would normally be as follows:

Hot water cylinder jacket These jackets are

available to suit all sizes of cylinder. To ensure you buy the correct size, measure the height and diameter of your cylinder. You should get a jacket that is at least 75 mm (3 in) thick and conforms to BS5615:1978. Some of the more recent cylinders have a built-in jacket of polyurethane foam around them and there is no need to insulate these further.

Each jacket will come with full fitting instructions. The main points to watch out for are that there are no gaps between the panels of the jacket when it is fitted and that you do not tighten the securing straps too much. If you do, you will reduce the thickness of the insulation and its

This is a typical example of draughtproofing a front door. Here a proprietary plastic and aluminium seal has been fitted, which runs all round the door frame. Details of this type of insulation are included in Chapter 5.

effectiveness. Remember not to cover the cap or cables leading to the immersion heater, if fitted.

In certain cases, grants are available for hot water cylinder jackets (see page 10).

Draughtproofing This is usually quite a cheap method of combatting heat loss and mainly involves sealing the gaps round windows and doors, although the floors may also require this treatment. Always start with the outside walls of the home and work inwards. Full details of types of draught excluders and how to fit them are included in Chapter 5.

Loft insulation If your house was built prior to 1978, it will almost certainly have less than the

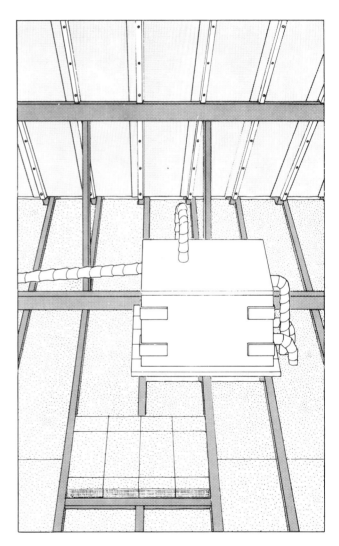

In this loft the floor has been insulated to the minimum recommended depth of 100 mm (4 in). This type of insulation is a relatively simple, inexpensive and highly effective means of reducing heat loss through the loft.

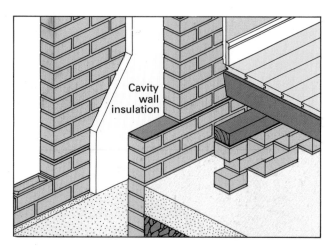

Cavity walls can be insulated with foam, polystyrene beads or glass or rock fibre. All provide efficient insulation and are very cost-effective. However, none are DIY jobs and must be left to a specialist contractor.

minimum recommended amount of loft floor insulation – which is currently 100 mm (or 4 in) thick. Depending on when it was built, the house may have no insulation at all.

This type of insulation is easy to lay and, because you can do it yourself, works out quite reasonably in terms of cost. Roof insulation will cost more and requires more work to fit, but will increase the insulation qualities of the loft space considerably and is very important if you are using the area for storage.

Remember that because a bungalow has more roof space in relation to the number of rooms than an ordinary house, it therefore needs loft insulation more than a house. Full details on what types of insulation to use and how to fit them are included in Chapter 2.

Cavity wall insulation If your house was built after 1920 but before 1978, it will probably have

uninsulated exterior cavity walls. Insulating these cavities is very cost-effective, but the work is not a DIY job and should always be carried out by a specialist. Make sure this carries a guarantee. If your home is made with solid or other non-cavity walls, there are alternative processes available to increase the insulation properties. Information of this area of

Secondary double glazing is available in a range of styles and finishes to suit all types of window. It is worth bearing in mind that the larger the window area, the more cost-effective the double glazing will be.

insulation is covered in Chapter 3.

Double glazing   There are several factors involved in the cost-effectiveness of double glazing. The most relevant is the amount of external wall space that is taken up with windows – and the size of individual windows. Double glazing will, for example, be more cost-effective fitted to large picture windows than small, cottage-type ones. The job of fitting double glazing can be done by one of the major glazing companies or a contractor. But you can buy DIY kits that will give you a very effective end-result. Double glazing is covered in Chapter 6.

Floor insulation   Whether your house has solid concrete floors or suspended timber ones fitted over ventilated cavities, considerable amounts of heat can be lost through them. Depending on the type of floor you have, there are various methods available for insulating them, which are discussed in Chapter 4.

Saving on heating costs

In addition to the savings you can make by installing the various forms of insulation discussed in this book, there are other general points to bear in mind that will help you to economise on the amount of fuel you use to heat the home.

1. If you have central heating controlled by a room thermostat, turn this down two or three degrees. While you will not notice the slight drop in the overall temperature, you will notice the saving in fuel used.

2. Check with your timer to see when the heating is programmed to switch on and off during each 24-hour period. There is no point in having the heating running all the time you are out of the house or in bed during the night. Also remember to adjust the timer at the start and finish of British Summer Time.

3. If you leave the house for more than a day during the winter months, adjust the controls so that your boiler switches on for just an hour each day at a lower than normal temperature. This precaution is to avoid the possibility of frost damage in severe weather.

4. There is no point in keeping the heating on in rooms you are 'airing' during the day. So if you throw open a bedroom window, turn off the heating in that room.

5. If you have an off-peak electricity meter in the home, for example for use with electric storage heaters, it is worth considering running the immersion heater on off-peak electricity too, if you have one fitted to your hot water storage cylinder.

6. Where you have radiators fitted in rooms that are

not used regularly, turn these off unless the rooms are being occupied.

7. One place in the home where considerable savings can be made in the use of hot water is the bathroom. If you do not already have a shower there, it is worth installing one since by using it instead of a bath you can save up to 45 litres (10 gall) of hot water per person.

8. Switch off any radiant heaters in rooms and hallways when not in use.

9. You will be surprised how much heat can be saved by hanging heavy curtains over windows and keeping them drawn across in cold winter evenings. Heavy drapes not only help keep in the warmth but also reduce draughts through the windows – and doors, for that matter.

10. Keep doors closed during the colder winter months. It is an obvious point, but one often forgotten, that all the time you stand talking in an open doorway heat is escaping and cold air entering.

11. Remember to close all internal doors as well. If you are keeping individual rooms or areas heated, there is no point in allowing that heat to escape to other areas not in use.

12. Repair any cracked or broken windows as soon as possible. Not only will you lose heat through these cracks, but they are also unsafe.

13. Make sure all gas and open fires and paraffin heaters have adequate ventilation when lit so that they burn correctly. Bear in mind, too, that one of the products of combustion is water vapour and if the area around these types of fire is not properly ventilated, condensation will form.

2 The roof and loft

The roof and loft space is one of the major potential areas for heat loss in the normal home – and the problem can be even greater in a single-storey building. It has been estimated that between 20% and 30% of all the heat lost in the average home passes through the roof. This is why it is such an important area to concentrate on when looking at where best to install insulation.

Before the 1960s few houses were fitted with any loft insulation. In fact it was regarded as quite a status symbol to have the snow melt off your roof first! You may have got rid of the snow, but just think how much heat you wasted in doing so.

Recommendations for insulation have increased over the years. In 1965 the figure was 25 mm (1 in) thickness of insulating material. This was increased to 50 mm (2 in) by 1974 and the most recent recommendation is for a layer 100 mm (4 in) thick. The signs are that the thickness of insulation will continue to be increased, particularly with the rising cost of fuel and the growing need to conserve energy resources.

Current regulations stipulate that with new houses there must be a minimum 100 mm (4 in) thick layer of insulation on the loft floor. This is, of course,

This is certainly not the view you want to see in your loft if you are anxious to conserve energy and cut down on fuel bills. There is no insulation between the joists and none round the storage cisterns or plumbing. Not only will up to 30% of the heat lost in the home escape through this area, but you will also run the risk of frozen and possibly burst pipes in very cold weather. Grants are available to help with the cost of insulation.

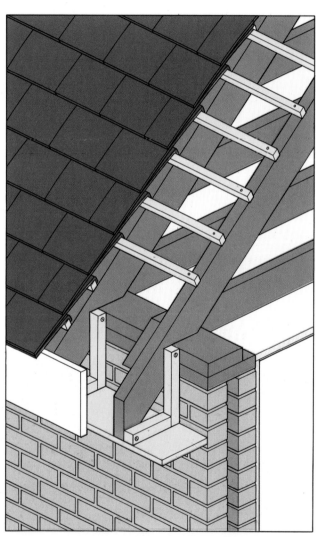

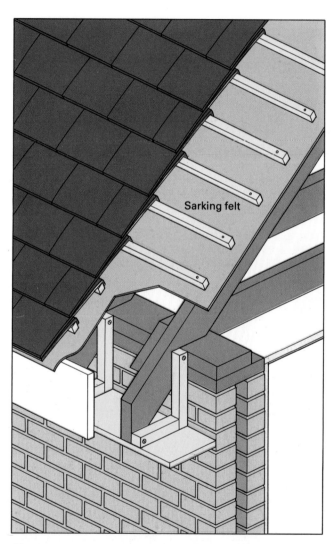

Sarking felt

Although insulation on the loft floor will go a long way to reducing heat losses, any roof that has not been felted or lined with boards, such as the one shown here, will have an effect on the overall insulation value of the loft.

Roofs that have been lined with sarking felt or boards, such as the one shown here, will have an increased insulation value, particularly since these types of lining will keep out most of the draughts and damp.

more than most older houses will have – if they have any at all. Grants are, however, available to help with insulating the loft area – and cutting an access flap if none exists (see page 10).

Naturally you should plan to follow the minimum requirement for insulation in the loft, but it may be worth considering increasing this amount to conserve even more heat, particularly in a bungalow. This you will have to decide on, bearing in mind the cost-effectiveness of the extra amount of insulation against the extra saving in fuel.

To do this, you will have to work out the cost of the heat loss through your roof (see pages 11–14). You should then balance this figure against the cost of insulation to the recommended thickness – 100 mm (4 in). The R value for this amount is 2.5. Next calculate the savings from thicker layers of insulation. If it is 140 mm (or 5½ in) thick, the R value is 3.5, while with 160 mm (or 6½ in) thick insulation the R value is 4.0. You can then assess the savings from thicker layers of insulation against the extra cost of materials over, say, a 10-year period.

One point you must bear in mind is the actual thickness of the insulation, which will determine the U value. If your ceiling joists are 100 mm (4 in) deep, any additional insulation will project over the top of these. If you subsequently lay down flooring in the loft or place heavy articles on top of the insulation, this will press it down and the U value will be reduced accordingly.

Although the floor area of a loft must be insulated, it is not the only area that needs this treatment. With modern houses that have tiled roofs, the tiles are laid over 2 mm (1/16 in) thick sarking felt or boards, which offer greater insulation and better draught and damp-proofing. With older properties, the tiles are hung on battens only, which are visible from the inside. These unlined roofs can lose up to 58% more heat than felted or boarded roofs and so it is important to ensure adequate insulation here too.

Before tackling any insulation job in the loft area, make sure you use a proprietary material that conforms to British Standard and has been approved by the Department of the Environment under the Homes Insulation Act. This is important, since it ensures that the material you use has the required insulation and thermal transmittance values – and the necessary fire-resistant properties.

A further point to remember is that you should not cover up electrical cables with insulation material. The heat generated by the passage of electrical current through a cable is normally dissipated into the air around the cable. If this cable is covered with insulation, overheating could occur and this could in turn affect the cable's insulation and create a fire hazard.

So make sure any electrical cables are lifted above granular or blanket insulation. Obviously that part of a cable running to a light fitting or switch will have

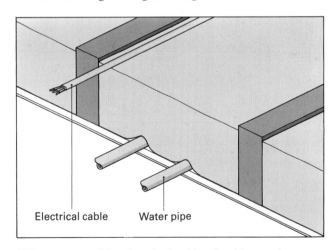

Electrical cable   Water pipe

Whenever possible, electrical cables should run above insulation material to allow any heat generated by the current passing through to dissipate into the air. Water pipes, conversely, should be buried in the insulation.

to pass through any insulation that has been installed.

Any water pipes running between joists will benefit from any insulation covering them. This will reduce the risk of water freezing and the possibility of a burst pipe in very cold weather.

Insulating the loft floor

The materials suitable for loft floor insulation fall into two main categories – granular and mineral fibre blanket.

Granular (loose-fill) insulation This type of floor insulation, which is supplied in large bags, consists of granules which you spread to the required depth around the loft floor between the joists. The main advantage of this type of insulation is that the granules can be spread easily into and around awkward areas and will loose-fill into relatively inaccessible spots. You will, of course, have to retain the granules at the edges of the loft to prevent the level sloping away and the granules falling down cavity walls.

Clear all movable objects from the loft. You will need a length of old plank or board on which to kneel while laying the granule – or blanket – insulation and this should be long enough to overlap two joists. This is important since if you put undue pressure on the ceiling between the joists it will give way. You must not use chipboard, since this may not be strong enough to carry your weight; if it breaks, the consequences could be disastrous.

Pour the granules between the joists. If the amount of insulation required is to the top of the joists, you can simply run a batten wide enough to span the joists along the top to level off the granules. If the required level is below the top of the joists, cut out a suitably sized 'T' shape in a board, so that the base of the 'T' is the required depth below the top of the joists. By running this T-shaped board along the

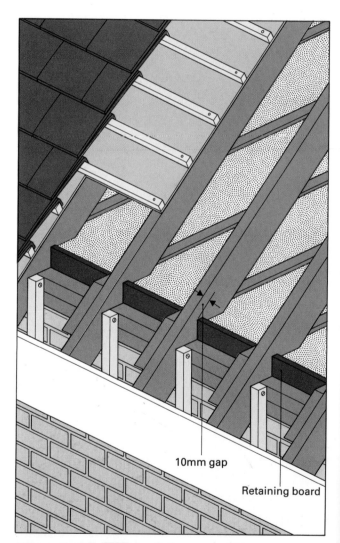

10mm gap

Retaining board

When using loose-fill insulation, you will have to fit retaining boards to prevent the granules falling into the cavity walls or under the eaves. But leave a gap of at least 10 mm (or $\frac{1}{2}$ in) around the edge for ventilation.

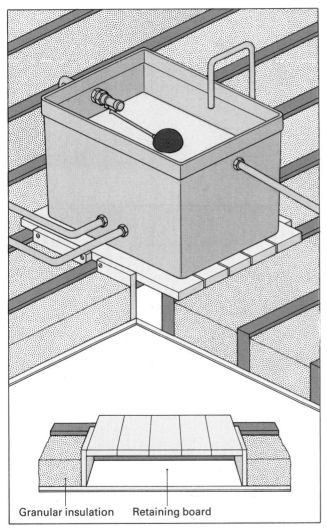

Granular insulation   Retaining board

The one area of the loft you should leave uninsulated is the floor under the cold water storage cistern to allow warm air from below to keep it from freezing. Again fit retaining boards if using loose-fill insulation.

joists, you will level off the granules at the depth you want. You should then press down the granules lightly with a large square piece of board fitted with a handle.

If you are laying granules right to the edge of the loft floor up to the eaves, make sure you fit strips of board round the edges between the joists to prevent the granules falling into the cavity walls or under the eaves. You must ensure, however, that there is a minimum 12 mm ($\frac{1}{2}$ in) gap all round the edges of the loft floor between the tile felt or board and the end of the insulation. This is to allow for air to ventilate the loft space. You should never seal it off completely, otherwise you will eventually get problems from condensation and damp.

There are two parts of the loft that should be left clear of insulation: under the cold water storage cistern and central heating expansion tank. The reason for this is that a certain amount of warm air should be allowed to come up from the heated rooms below to prevent the cistern or tank from freezing up in very cold weather. When using granules, you will have to fix lengths of board around the bottom of the cistern or tank to prevent the insulation running underneath (see diagram).

Granules can be used in conjunction with the blanket-type of insulation, where there are awkward areas such as odd gaps and corners and round the chimney. Equally, you will not be able to insulate the loft flap or door with granules and in this case you will need to use a piece of the blanket-type insulation instead.

Manufacturers give guidance as to the amount of granules you will need to cover a specific area. As a guide, however, one bag should cover an area of 5 sq m (50 sq ft) to a depth of 25 mm (1 in). To work out the rough area of your loft, you will find it much easier to measure the outside of your house. Check on the width and length and then multiply these figures together.

Blanket insulation This type of insulation is available in two main forms – rock fibre, which is made from inorganic rock fibres, and glass fibre – and both are available in various widths and thicknesses. Manufacturers issue tables showing the number of rolls of insulation required, depending on the floor area of the loft. Make sure you buy the correct width to fit between the joists. Again, the easiest way to measure the area of the loft is from the outside of the house.

When you buy the rolls of blanket insulation, you will find that the material when rolled is about half the thickness you ordered. This is because it is compression-packed to save space. The blanket should expand to the correct thickness when you unroll it.

Make sure you have handy a sharp kitchen knife, a large pair of scissors and a roll of tape or ball of string. You may need a light in the loft, which you can run from downstairs with an extension lead if you do not ready have one fitted.

Glass fibre can irritate the skin and will get into clothes. So wear old clothing and put on a pair of rubber gloves to protect your hands. Carry the rolls of blanket insulation into the loft before you undo them. As you discard the wrapping, make sure you do not leave it lying around so it gets trapped underneath.

Always start at the corner furthest from the loft flap or door and work back towards it. Unroll the insulation and fit it down between the joists up to the eaves. Make sure, however, that you leave a gap of about 12 mm ($\frac{1}{2}$ in) – or 25 mm (1 in) if the pitch of the roof is less than 15 degrees – between the edge of the insulation and the underside of the roof felt to allow for ventilation. Work back to the middle of the loft and then start again from the other side.

Where the two lengths meet, approximately in the middle of the loft, make sure you cut them to overlap by about 50 mm (2 in), then butt-join the ends.

When laying blanket insulation, always start from the edge and work towards the centre. Remember to leave a 10 mm (or $\frac{1}{2}$ in) gap by the eaves for ventilation.

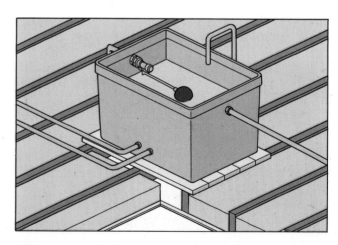

When you reach the area around the cold water storage cistern, trim the blanket insulation so that it lays up to the sides of the cistern. The same, of course, applies if you have an expansion tank for the central heating.

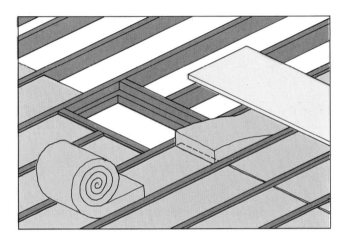

Where you have to join lengths of insulation, make sure that the ends are butted tightly together to prevent any heat leaking through the gap.

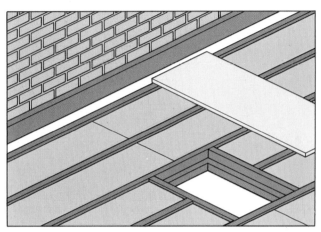

To cope with the narrow gap between the end joists and the end walls of the house, you will have to cut strips of insulation to size with some sharp scissors.

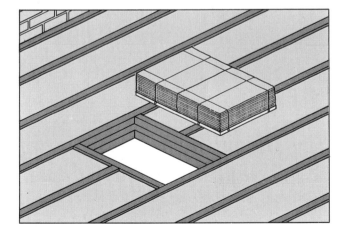

One area that tends to be overlooked is the loft flap. You will have to use blanket insulation here. Cut out a piece the correct size and secure it to the flap with either tape or string.

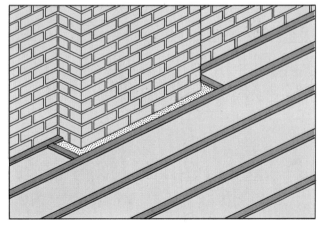

In awkward areas where it would be difficult to lay blanket insulation, you can use loose-fill instead. When you pour this into the small gaps, make sure it is to the same level as the rest of the insulation.

Continue this method until all the strips of insulation have been laid and check that they have expanded to their correct depth. If not, the material is not up to specification and you should return it to your suppliers.

There is normally a narrow gap between the outside joists and the external walls of the house and you can insulate this with offcuts of blanket when you have finished insulating the main area.

Remember that you must leave the area under the cold water storage cistern and the central heating expansion tank uninsulated to prevent the possibility of the water freezing.

One area that is often missed out is the loft flap or door. You can only use blanket insulation here and this should be cut to size and then fixed on with tape or string (see diagram on page 29).

No doubt you will come across those awkward areas where it is very difficult to lay blanket insulation effectively. Here it is best to use granules. Make sure you lay these to the correct depth.

Insulating the storage cistern

Kits of expanded polystyrene panels are available to lag most types of storage cistern and central heating expansion tanks. You should make a suitably shaped lid out of chipboard to cover the top and cut holes through which the return pipes can pass. If you

Here you can see the loft floor completely insulated with blanket material. When you are covering the loft flap, it is a good idea to wrap the insulation in polythene to prevent hands being irritated when the flap is opened.

When insulating the cold water storage cistern with glass fibre, first bind the strips of wrap round all the pipes connecting to the cistern and hold the ends in place with PVC tape. Do not cover up any taps or valves.

To insulate the cistern, first cover the top and sides with lengths of glass fibre blanket to meet the insulation between the joists on the loft floor.

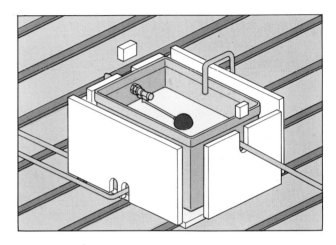

You can, of course, insulate the cold water storage cistern with polystyrene panels. Cut these to cover the sides, making sure they fit neatly round the pipes.

Having put the lengths of glass fibre over the top and sides, cut and position pieces at either end, making slits to feed the insulation over the connecting pipes, then secure all pieces lightly with lengths of string – or tape.

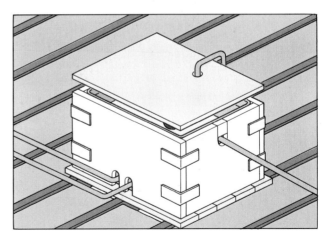

Having secured all the side panels in place with tape, cut the top piece to fit and rest it on the side pieces. You will have to cut a hole to take the vent pipe from the domestic hot water system.

prefer, or cannot find a suitable kit, you can use blanket insulation to lag the cistern or tank.

Cut sufficient lengths off the insulation roll to cover the sides and top of the cistern with separate pieces for the ends. To secure the pieces round the cistern, tie them with lengths of tape or string (see pictures). Do not pull these too tight or you will cut into the insulation and reduce its effectiveness.

When you have finished, take all the paper wrapping out of the loft. To avoid any irritation from bits of glass fibre, hold your hands and arms under a cold water tap for a minute or two and then wash them thoroughly. You should also wash the clothing you were wearing in case any glass fibres are caught on it.

Insulating the plumbing

While you are insulating the loft, this is a perfect opportunity to check that the plumbing system is properly lagged as well. Because the insulation will make the loft that much colder, it is even more important that all pipes are lagged to prevent the possibility of them freezing. These will include the supply pipes to and from the cistern or tank, the valves and the overflow pipes.

The easiest method is to use split foam lagging which you simply wrap over the exposed lengths of pipe. This must be 25 mm (1 in) thick and is available in different diameters, depending on the size of pipe to be lagged. You can either secure the split foam with PVC tape or, better still, use the type with a zip fastener. When lagging valves, wrap odd bits of insulation round the fittings and hold them in place with PVC tape. Make sure the valves can still be turned.

The cistern or tank will have a supply pipe and at least one feed pipe from the bottom. There will also be a pipe ending in a 'U' bend over the top of the

cistern or tank and an overflow pipe running from near the top to the outside of the house. Although the last two pipes will not normally have water in them, they still need to be lagged as a safety precaution. In the event of a fault in the plumbing or heating system, water might be passing slowly through them. The danger would then be that they might freeze up in severe weather if unprotected. This could result in serious flooding.

Flooring the loft

Having insulated the floor of the loft, using one of the methods described, you may find you have a problem when it comes to storing heavy items in the loft space. The difficulty is that any heavy object placed on top of the insulation material will compress

The simplest method of lagging the plumbing pipes is by using the split foam insulation which you just wrap over the pipe and fasten. Make sure you get the correct diameter for the pipes you are lagging.

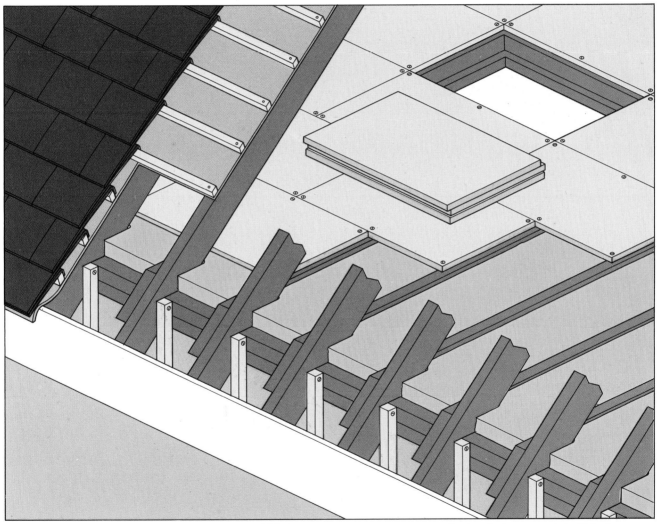

When flooring the loft, you should use 20 mm ($\frac{3}{4}$ in) thick chipboard or shuttering plywood. Lay it in strips or panels, fixing these with either nails or screws along their edges to the centre of the joists. The new flooring must not compress the insulation material. If it does, you will have to fix extra lengths of timber onto the joists to raise the level of the flooring. Do not block the ventilation gap around the edge of the loft.

33

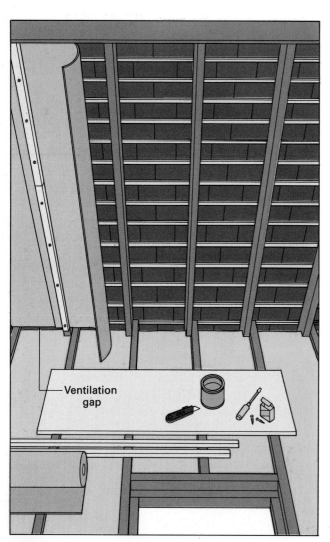

Ventilation gap

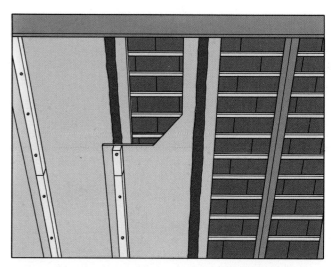

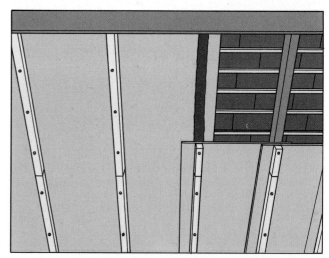

Here you can see the stages involved in felting the roof between the rafters. The strips of sarking felt are held in place with timber battens. Measure up and cut these strips and pre-drill the batten fixing holes before you take the material into the loft. Seal all the gaps along the fixing edges of the felt with cold bitumastic adhesive to improve the insulation and cut out draughts. Use screws for fixing to prevent disturbing the tiles.

it and reduce its insulation value. If you are going to use the loft for this type of storage, you will have to lay down flooring.

You can do this using either 20 mm (or $\frac{3}{4}$ in) thick chipboard or shuttering plywood, which should be cut into manageable strips or rectangles the same width as the centres of the joists (that is the distance from the middle of one joist to the middle of the next). Fix these strips on to the joists using 50 mm (2 in) oval nails or No 10 countersunk screws.

When laying flooring in the loft, you must again remember that the insulation should not be compressed. If it does not come above the top of the joists, there is no problem. If it does, then you will have to increase the height of all the joists by nailing on extra lengths of timber so that the flooring material is above the insulation when fixed in place.

It is worth remembering that the flooring will improve the insulation in the loft. For example, 20 mm ($\frac{3}{4}$ in) thick plywood has an R value of 0.42.

Insulating the roof

With some older houses, the chances are that there is no felt beneath the roof tiles. Even where it has been fitted, you should check to make sure it is still intact and does not need replacing.

If necessary, you can either fit felt or strips of hardboard beneath the tiles. This will not only improve the insulation of your loft but will also cut down on draughts and dirt being blown about inside. These precautions are even more essential if you are considering using the loft for storage.

It is also worth bearing in mind that by keeping the temperature of the loft area higher, you will reduce the amount of heat passing through the floor insulation.

You can fit either felt or hardboard – but not both. The reason for this is that if you install felt beneath the tiles and then cover over the rafters with hardboard, the gap between the two will not be sufficiently ventilated and you are likely to experience problems from mould or rot later on.

Lining with felt You need to use 2 mm ($\frac{1}{16}$ in) thick black roofing felt – not the green felt with chippings. It is best to fit the felt in warm conditions when the material is not so brittle and you can cut it more easily. Use a large pair of scissors, a cutting knife or an old panel saw. The felt is quite messy to handle, so wear an old pair of gloves. The black deposit from it is not easy to remove from tools, hands or clothing, but the best way to get it off is to use a paint thinner or neat washing-up liquid.

Cut the felt into suitable length strips about 200 mm (or 8 in) wider than the gaps between the rafters. Fix the overlapping felt on either side to each rafter using 35 × 12 mm ($1\frac{1}{2} \times \frac{1}{2}$ in) battens, which you should screw to the rafters. Use 32 mm ($1\frac{1}{4}$ in) No 8 zinc-plated screws, spacing them at about 450 mm (18 in) intervals. Do not nail these battens in place since the impact from the hammer could dislodge the tiles and your roof will then leak.

Make sure when you fix the felt that you leave a gap of at least 12 mm ($\frac{1}{2}$ in) between the felt and the tiles to allow air to circulate. Overlap any joins in the felt by at least 75 mm (3 in) and seal these joins with a recommended bitumastic adhesive.

Work your way round the roof until you have filled in all the gaps between the rafters. Remember not to fit the felt tight to the loft floor insulation, since there should be a slight gap at the eaves to provide ventilation.

Lining with hardboard This job is a lot cleaner than using roofing felt. You should fit 3 mm ($\frac{1}{8}$ in) thick tempered hardboard. You can buy this in 2440 × 1220 mm (8 × 4 ft) sheets. You will need to cut each sheet into smaller workable pieces or strips and it is worth making friends with your timber supplier and getting him to cut these up for you. Measure the

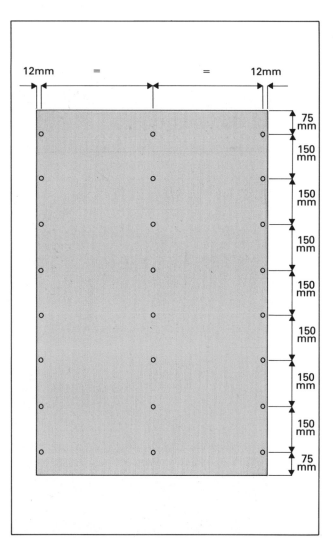

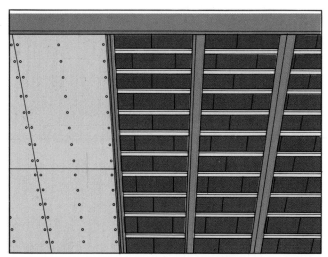

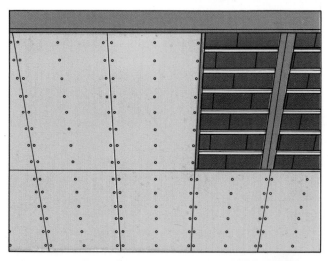

As an alternative to sarking felt, you can line the roof across the rafters with sections of hardboard, as shown here. Carefully measure up and pre-drill the fixing holes before you take the hardboard into the loft. You will find the sections are easier to fit if you keep them to a manageable size. Screw the sections in place, butting adjoining edges tightly together over the centre of the rafters. Remember to leave a gap just above the floor.

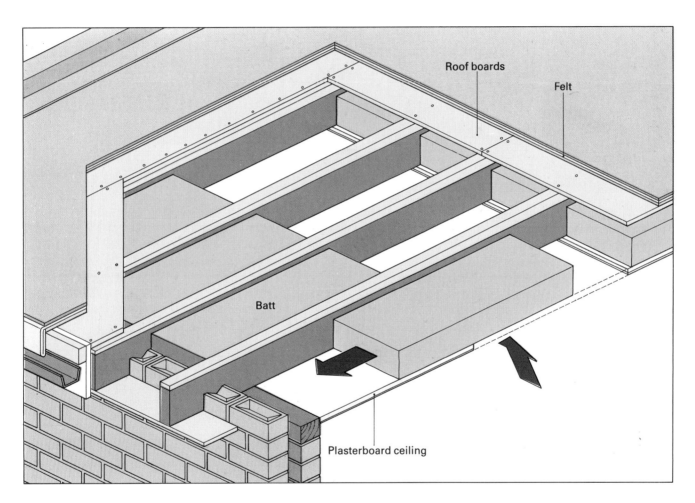

Roof boards

Felt

Batt

Plasterboard ceiling

When insulating a flat roof, you will have to remove a section of the ceiling across the width of each room to provide access to the roof space. Cut the lengths of insulation to size and slide them carefully between the joists. Make sure when you do this that you do not disturb any electrical wiring above the ceiling, in particular the overhead light fittings. You will have to insulate in the gap you have made for access. You can hold the insulation in position by tacking lengths of string between joists and resting the length on these, until you have filled the gap with plasterboard. You must leave a slight gap above the insulation and below the roof to allow for ventiliation. When filling the gap in the ceiling, seal the edges before redecorating.

distance between the centres of the rafters so that he can cut the sheets to the right widths.

You can either fix the hardboard in strips between adjacent rafters or in sections across three rafters. But bear in mind that the larger the span, the harder the job of fixing will be.

When you fix the sections of hardboard to the rafters, use screws and not nails to prevent the possibility of dislodging the tiles. You will need 25 mm (1 in) No 6 countersunk rustproof screws and these should be spaced at about 150 mm (or 6 in) intervals along the edges of the hardboard. Pre-drill holes in the hardboard approximately 12 mm ($\frac{1}{2}$ in) in from the edges and then fix the sections of hardboard to the rafters. The edges should come in the centre of each rafter, so that you allow enough fixing area for the next piece.

You will have to trim the edges of the hardboard where necessary to fit around those areas where other roofing timbers cross the rafters.

Start at the awkward part of the roof, from the eaves up, and remember to leave a small gap – 12–25 mm ($\frac{1}{2}$–1 in) – between the floor insulation and the bottom edges of the hardboard to ensure sufficient ventilation. Do not fix the hardboard below the level of the floor insulation.

Insulating flat roofs

Many extensions are now built with flat, boarded and felted roofs. Those put up recently should already have sufficient insulation fitted between the plasterboard ceiling and the underside of the chipboard roof. Once installed, this type of roof will be difficult to insulate since the work would involve either removing the roof or the plasterboard ceiling.

There are two basic methods of increasing the insulation value of a flat roof. One is to add an extra roof above the existing one using insulated roofing boards. These can be bought pre-felted; otherwise you must fix three layers of exterior roofing felt over them. This can be a major job and you should seek the advice of a qualified local builder or your local planning office before attempting any alteration.

The second method (see diagram on page 37) involves removing a section of the ceiling right across the underside of the roof and inserting rigid rock or glass fibre or expanded polystyrene panels, also called batts, between the joists. You will have to slide the insulation material into place through the gap.

Take care when inserting these slabs that you do not interfere with or damage any light fittings or wiring in the ceiling. To avoid any possible problems, you may find it easier to cut any affected slabs into two pieces and fit these either side of the wiring or fitting.

If you use this method, make sure you do not fill the gap completely, since you must allow for ventilation. Before replacing the section of the ceiling you had to remove, do not forget to insulate that area of the ceiling as well.

Using contractors

If you are unwilling – or unable – to carry out your own loft insulation, there are many specialist contractors available to do the work for you. If you are in a position to claim a grant for this work, a certain amount will be allocated towards labour costs, thus reducing the overall expense. Make sure, however, that any contractor you use is working to the Code of Practice laid down by the Association of Insulation Contractors and the relevant British Standards.

3 The walls

The largest single area of heat loss in most homes is the walls. This may not, of course, apply in a bungalow, where the roof is the major offender since there is normally double the roof area for the same number of rooms as a two-storey house. It is most important to ensure that the walls are sufficiently well insulated if you are to make significant savings in fuel costs.

This means that the U factor of the walls must be as low as possible. Current building regulations stipulate that the minimal thermal transmittance value for external walls of any dwelling must not exceed 0.6 w/m² °C. In other words, the U value of your external walls should not be more than 0.6. It is generally recognised that between 0.4 and 0.5 is the best figure to aim at.

Single glazed windows can be a major cause of heat loss, particularly in older properties, and it is estimated that on average something like 25% of domestic heat is lost through the windows.

This can be as much as halved with double glazing and halved again with triple glazing – or with the new low emissivity coated glass which, when used in double glazing, gives a similar thermal performance to that achieved with triple glazing (see page 105).

The U values for typical external wall constructions are as follows:

Material	U value
225 mm (or 9 in) solid brick wall	2.1
Cavity wall – brick outer leaf/50 mm (2 in) uninsulated cavity/breeze block inner leaf/9.5 mm (⅜ in) plasterboard	1.37
Cavity wall – brick outer leaf/50 mm (2 in) uninsulated cavity/concrete block inner leaf/9.5 mm (⅜ in) plasterboard	0.96
Cavity wall – brick outer leaf/50 mm (2 in) uninsulated cavity/112 mm (4½ in) insulating block inner leaf/9.5 mm (⅜ in) plasterboard	0.57
Cavity wall – brick outer leaf/50 mm (2 in) insulated cavity/100 mm (4 in) insulating block/12 mm (½ in) lightweight plaster	0.43
Timber-clad 200 mm (8 in) insulating block with 12 mm (½ in) lightweight plaster	0.6

From these figures you will see that most houses built before the mid-1970s have poorly insulated external walls. With more recently built houses, the external walls will either have insulated cavities or solid insulating blocks to meet the current requirements.

Cavity walls

With new houses, modern building techniques include cavity insulation, using slabs of insulating material of a suitable thickness, built into the walls. Because of the process involved, it is impossible to fit this type of insulation to existing buildings. There are, however, several methods available to insulate cavity walls of buildings not originally treated in this way. But these types of insulation are not DIY jobs and require specialist treatment and equipment from a qualified contractor.

Foam insulation With the introduction of cavity wall foam insulation (using urea formaldehyde foam) many small firms were set up to install it, with mixed results. Unless this type of insulation is properly installed, there can be serious problems not only from the point of view of expense, where damp has been able to penetrate, but also from the safety aspect, where excessive fumes have found their way inside the house.

As a result, a British Standard was drawn up both for the urea formaldehyde foam and also the method

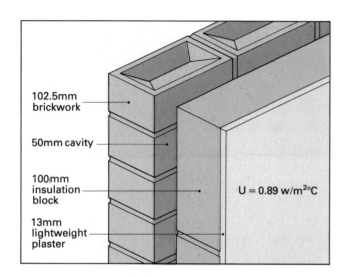

102.5mm brickwork

50mm cavity

100mm insulation block

13mm lightweight plaster

U = 0.89 w/m²°C

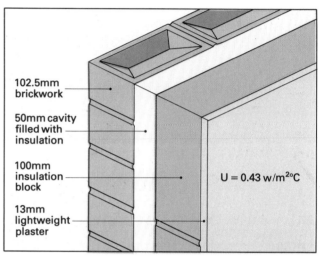

102.5mm brickwork

50mm cavity filled with insulation

100mm insulation block

13mm lightweight plaster

U = 0.43 w/m²°C

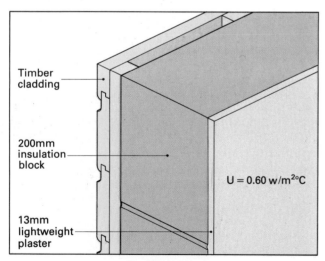

Timber cladding

200mm insulation block

13mm lightweight plaster

U = 0.60 w/m²°C

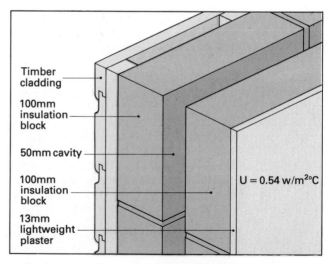

Timber cladding

100mm insulation block

50mm cavity

100mm insulation block

13mm lightweight plaster

U = 0.54 w/m²°C

Four different types of external wall construction with their relative U values. The one top left is probably the most common type of cavity wall construction. By insulating the cavity (top right) you can reduce the U value by more than 50%. Above left shows a frequently used method for cladding walls, using timber or tiles over thick insulation blocks. You can clad cavity walls with timber (above), but insulation here is more difficult.

of installation (BS 5617 and 5618). A special surveillance scheme has also been set up by the British Standards Institute under which firms installing this type of insulation can register. It is definitely in your interest to ensure that the firm you decide to use to install cavity wall insulation is registered under this scheme. For one reason, it guarantees that the insulation will be correctly and safely installed.

Only those firms registered under the scheme are allowed to install foam insulation in cavities between inner and outer leaves of masonry without local authority scrutiny.

Make sure you obtain several quotations for the work before making your choice. Check, too, with neighbours in your road as to whether they are considering having a similar insulation installed, since some firms offer a discount where more than one house in the immediate area wants the same type of insulation.

The insulation itself is a mixture of urea formaldehyde resin, hardener and water with a foaming agent, which is injected under pressure through a set of pre-drilled holes in the outer leaf of the outside walls into the cavity. As it is injected, the resin foams up inside the cavity and then sets hard. The material and the trapped air around it provide an excellent insulation barrier which considerably lowers the U value of the treated walls.

However, foam is not a suitable type of insulation for all types of walls. If both leaves of the wall are of masonry construction, there should be no problems in using this treatment. If your walls are of a different construction, such as weatherboard or Dutch tile, you may be able to use the foam insulation method, but permission will need to be sought from the local authority. Your contractor should arrange this for you. You are also required to inform the local authority before the work starts and, here again, the contractor should do this. But, as a

Foam insulation is ideal for houses of masonry cavity wall construction. Holes are drilled into the outer leaf of the outside walls and the foam insulation is then injected through them under pressure.

41

check, always ask to see a copy of the official notification.

As a general rule, this type of cavity wall insulation should work out cheaper than other forms of wall insulation, provided of course it is suitable for the type of house construction you have and that it is correctly installed.

Other cavity wall insulation Where foam insulation is not suitable – or if you would prefer not to have that material installed – there are other fillings available which will insulate cavity walls.

Expanded polystyrene beads or other granular materials can be blown through pre-drilled holes into the cavity of an external wall. With some processes,

the material is coated with adhesive so the beads or granules stick together after they have been injected into the cavity, thus completely trapping air inside and making the whole mass stable.

Another material that is used for this kind of insulation is mineral fibre. The basic substance is a special type of rock or glass, which is melted and then spun into very fine fibres. Like the foam and granules, these fibres are also blown into the cavity through pre-drilled holes.

Whether you choose the granule or fibre method of insulation, a scheme exists to control the material and workmanship and ensure that they meet current building regulations. It is controlled by the Agrement

Cavity walls can be insulated with expanded polystyrene beads. In order to inject this material into the cavity, holes have to be drilled in the outer leaf of the wall. This is done through the mortar joints.

The expanded polystyrene beads, which are coated with adhesive to form a cohesive mass and prevent seepage or spillage, are injected through the drilled holes. These are then sealed with a matching mortar.

Board and only approved firms can register. Always ask to see an Agrement Board Certificate from your contractor. Make sure before you commit yourself that both the method and the contractor satisfy the minimum requirements.

One point you should bear in mind when choosing cavity wall insulation is whether any cables that regularly carry a heavy current pass through or run down this cavity. The sort of cables you should be checking on are those supplying a cooker, immersion heater or storage heaters, for example.

The reason for checking on these is that the power rating for cables assumes that they are normally exposed to the air, enabling the heat generated from the passage of electricity through the cables to dissipate into the surrounding air. Should any cable be encased in foam insulation, for example, the heat will not be able to dissipate so easily. In extreme cases, this could cause a breakdown in the cable insulation through overheating, leading to a short circuit and possibly fire.

It is therefore a wise precaution to tell your contractor if such cable runs exist. If these cables regularly carry loads up to the recommended maximum, you would be well advised to replace them with the next larger size of cable to reduce the possibility of overheating.

Solid walls

If the property you live in is built with solid external walls rather than double-leaf cavity ones, it is still possible to insulate these and improve the U value. You can either fit insulating material on the outside or the inside of the wall – or both. There are advantages and disadvantages in both methods. One common factor, however, is that unfortunately they both cost more to install than cavity wall insulation.

As a rule, outside insulation is usually more difficult to install but obviously does not cause as much disruption and inconvenience as you would suffer if the work was on the inside of the wall. If by using the exterior method the appearance of the outside of the house will be altered, you should check with your local authority before going ahead with the work, since any change in appearance may not comply with local by-laws.

You will not normally require this permission when treating the inside of the wall. Bear in mind, however, that by insulating inside you will be reducing the size of your rooms and the existence of adjoining walls, floors and ceilings will create extra work – and possibly problems.

Another method of insulating cavity walls uses mineral fibre. This material is blown into the cavity again through the holes drilled in the outer leaf of the outside walls. In this case the insulation used is glass fibre.

External insulation Insulating the outside of walls is expensive, even if you do it yourself. The chances are that it will involve altering window frames, sills and door frames. You will probably have to resite rainwater pipes as well so the job is best done by professionals. Unless you are considering having the outside of the house re-rendered, it is unlikely to be cost-effective.

Various types of insulation are available using glass or rock fibres and some have a steel mesh fixed to the outside to give extra strength. Other systems include the use of such materials as polystyrene, polyurethane, foamed glass and polyisocyanurate. The insulation comes in panels, which should be fixed to the outside walls above the level of the damp proof course, or can be added as small beads to the render.

There are a number of systems specially designed for external insulation and more information can be obtained from the External Wall Insulation Association.

Internal insulation There are several advantages in insulating the inside of the walls rather than the outside. By forming an insulation barrier between the room and the wall you will effectively reduce the amount of heat absorbed by the wall. This means that the room will heat up more quickly, although of course it will lose heat more quickly too when the heating is switched off.

Internal insulation is cheaper to install than exterior insulation and you can spread the cost and aggravation by treating rooms individually. Outside, the whole job has to be done at one go.

The more costly yet more effective methods of insulating the inside of the walls do involve reducing the size of the room being treated. Other work involved includes altering the position of internal window sills, door frames, electrical wall socket outlets, switches and wall lights, since you will be increasing the thickness of the walls in each room.

There is a range of insulation available to treat walls inside. All help reduce the U value of external walls and we will look at the most complicated and expensive through to the simplest and cheaper methods. All methods will involve redecorating the affected walls after the insulation has been installed.

Two basic methods can be used to fit insulation on the inside of walls. The first is to make up a timber framework using 25 or 50 mm (1 or 2 in) thick battens and then fit plasterboard sheets on to the framework. The cavity created behind the plasterboard should be filled with insulating material, such as glass or rock fibre building roll or expanded polystyrene sheets.

The second method is to stick thermal board on to your existing wall. This board is, in fact, plasterboard with an expanded polystyrene or polyurethane foam backing.

Both methods will give you approximately the same insulation value, thickness for thickness. The first is probably best used on walls that are uneven or damaged, since the second requires a sound, flat surface on which to bond the thermal board. With either method you must make sure that the walls to be lined are sound and free from damp before you carry out the work.

Using a batten framework

You must first decide on the thickness of the insulation you require, since this will determine the size of battens you use to make up the framework. Glass or rock fibre building roll is available in thicknesses of 20, 50, 60, 80 or 100 mm ($\frac{3}{4}$, 2, $2\frac{3}{8}$, $3\frac{3}{16}$ or 4 in). Polystyrene sheets, which measure 2440 × 1220 mm (8 × 4 ft), come in thicknesses of 12.5, 19 and 25 mm ($\frac{1}{2}$, $\frac{3}{4}$ and 1 in). Your battens must therefore be as thick as the insulation you use and 50 mm (2 in) wide to give you sufficient fixing

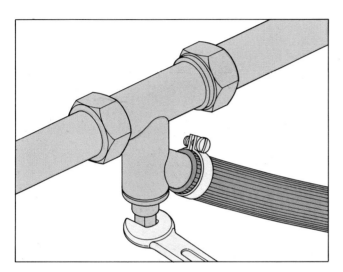

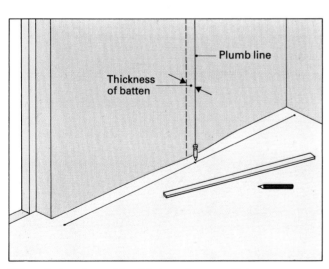

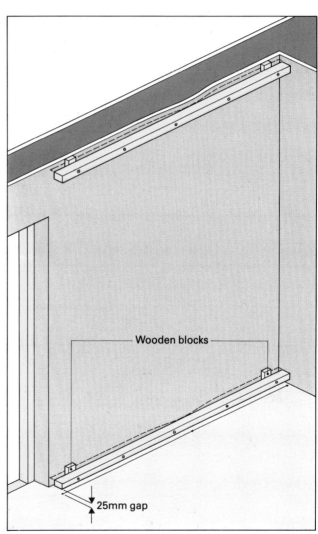

When lining the walls with board, you will have to
remove any radiators. Before doing this, drain the water
in the system via a hosepipe attached to the draincock
(top left). You will find that walls are rarely perfectly

straight, and you should always mark the position of the
batten framework on the floor and ceiling from the 'high
point' (above left). When fitting the top and bottom
battens, use packing pieces to hold them level (above).

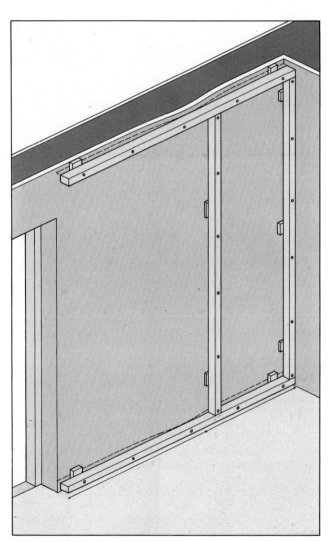

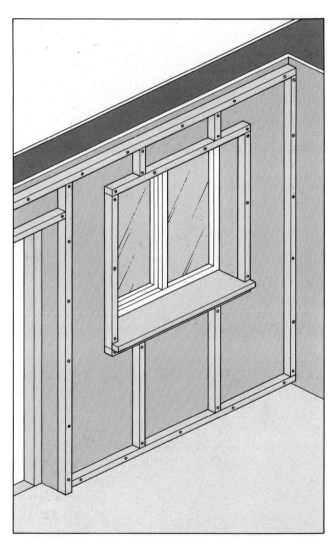

Having fitted the top and bottom lengths of batten to the wall, you can now screw the vertical battens in position. Make sure that the front face of each is flush with the front face of the horizontal battens and use

packing pieces as required to hold the battens rigid. You will also have to fix battens round any window and door opening. Adjustments may be necessary to tackle sills. Here the sill projects over the batten.

surface for the plasterboard panels.

Fitting the framework   The first job is to clear the wall surface. This means removing the skirting boards and door architraves, which should be eased off the wall in a similar manner, and fixtures that are screwed to the wall and all electrical fittings such as sockets, switches and wall lights. All items to be fitted back on the wall will need their own batten framework on which they can be mounted afterwards (see diagram opposite).

You will also have to disconnect any radiators on the wall and remove them, which will involve draining the hot water system first. Turn off the boiler and connect a hosepipe to the draincock fitted at the lowest point on the heating circuit. Turn off the main stopcock controlling the flow into the rising main, which will usually be located in the kitchen under the sink. Make sure the hosepipe feeds outside the house so that you do not flood the area around the draincock and then open this draincock. Once you have drained the system, do not switch on any form of water heating until you have reconnected the radiators and refilled the system.

It may be possible to blank off the pipe ends either side of any affected radiator and refill the system temporarily while you are installing the insulation. But unless you are experienced in tackling work on the plumbing system, you should consult a qualified plumber before you attempt this.

Having stripped the wall of all fixtures and fittings, scrape off any loose or damaged plaster or wallpaper. You will now need to check on whether the wall is straight. Unfortunately very few are. Using a plumb bob and line, at various points along the wall, find the point at which the line hangs closest to the wall (see diagram). Move it out from the wall the same distance as the thickness of the battens you are using and mark on the floor and ceiling where the line hangs. Repeat this procedure at both ends of the wall as well so that you can draw a

straight line on both the floor and ceiling to correspond with the outside edge of the batten framework when fitted.

One point to bear in mind here is that you will have to roll back any carpet you have on the floor and trim the edges up to the new wall line when the insulation is fitted in place. If you have carpet tiles, lift the last one in each row and trim them to size before replacing them when the job is finished. You should not have to worry about vinyl or hard floor coverings.

Having made sure all the battens are treated with a wood preservative, first fit the bottom line of battens to the bottom of the wall 25 mm (1 in) up from the floor. Fix them with No 10 countersunk screws at about 450 mm (18 in) intervals, having first drilled and plugged suitable fixing holes in the wall. The screws should be long enough to allow at least 20 mm ($\frac{3}{4}$ in) of each to screw into the wall. Always drill holes in the battens first and then mark through these on to the wall to ensure the holes are drilled into the wall in the correct positions. If the wall surface is not even, you will have to insert small pieces of wood as packing where there are gaps behind the battens to ensure they remain straight. Now fix battens in a similar manner to the top of the wall 25 mm (1 in) down from the ceiling.

The next stage is to fix the vertical battens. Mark their position on the wall, spacing them at 600 mm (2 ft) intervals. Using a long straight-edge, check that each batten when fixed in place is flush with the surface of the horizontal battens already fitted. Then use the same method to screw these battens to the wall.

You will, of course, have to fit additional battens round the edges of all window frames and door openings to bring the surrounds out to the new wall surface. These battens must be fitted so they are flush with the edges of the reveals and will need to have their exposed surface planed down, since you

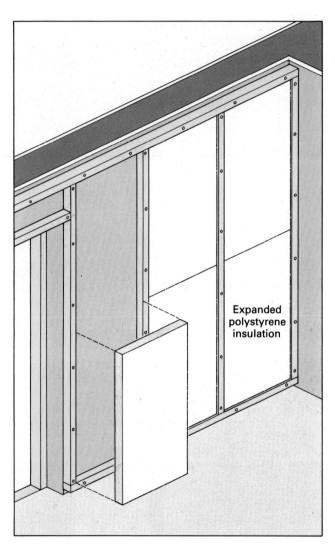

Expanded
polystyrene
insulation

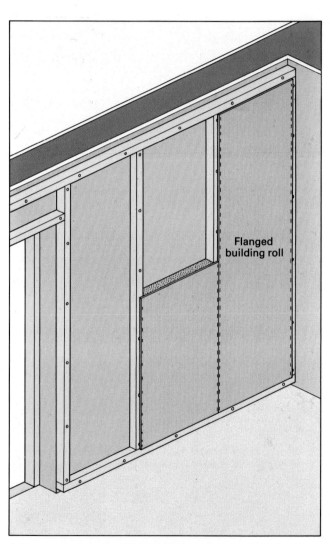

Flanged
building roll

If you are using polystyrene to insulate behind boards, the sections must fit snugly between the battens. Cut them to size with a fine-toothed hacksaw blade against a metal straight-edge, preferably outside.

If you are using flanged building roll as insulation, fit lengths between the battens and secure in place with either tacks or staples, fixing these at intervals of 150 mm (6 in) down each side of the lengths.

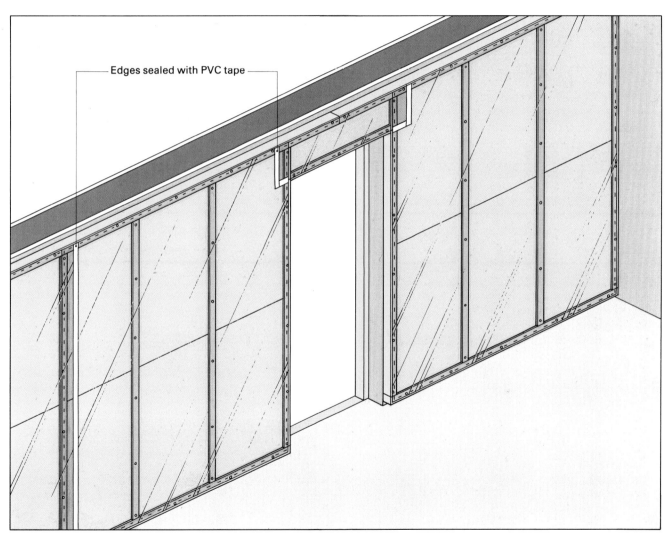

Edges sealed with PVC tape

Whether you are using polystyrene or flanged building roll, you will need to fit a polythene vapour barrier to prevent condensation forming in the insulation. Fix sections of this sheet with either tacks or staples, sealing all joints with PVC tape. Where holes have to be made through which to feed pipes or electrical cables, these must also be sealed with PVC tape. Check carefully that there are no tears or splits in the polythene.

will be decorating this later. If the room is higher than the length of the sheets of plasterboard, you must fit additional horizontal battens where individual sheets have to be joined.

Fitting the insulation If you are using expanded polystyrene as insulation, you will have to cut this to size to get a push-fit between the battens. You can do this with a fine-toothed hacksaw blade against a metal straight-edge, but it is advisable to cut the polystyrene outside, since the 'dust' you get when you cut is very difficult to clean up.

Glass or rock fibre building roll can be easily cut to size with a large pair of scissors. Stick this insulation to the wall with a suitable adhesive; your supplier will advise you on the type to use. If you get the flanged building roll, you can staple the edges to the battens.

When you have fitted all the insulation, cover the whole wall with a layer of 250 gauge polythene sheet. This will give you a vapour barrier to prevent condensation forming in the insulation. This barrier must be complete, so overlap lengths by at least 75 mm (3 in) and seal all edges with PVC tape. Where electrical cable or pipes have to penetrate the vapour barrier, seal round them with PVC tape.

Fitting the plasterboard You must now cut lengths of plasterboard to fit on to the framework over the insulation. Measure the height of the wall for each length of board and cut it to size, allowing a 12 mm ($\frac{1}{2}$ in) gap top and bottom. Offer each length up to the wall to check for fit and mark and cut any holes necessary to take electrical fittings or pipes.

Plasterboard is quite brittle and does not bend, so you should be careful when handling it. Always carry sheets edge-on and do not let anything fall on to the surface, since it can dent easily. Working from the ivory side of the board, cut each length to shape with a fine-toothed saw. To cut out holes, use a padsaw or hacksaw blade. To remove any paper burrs, lightly rub down all cut edges with fine glasspaper.

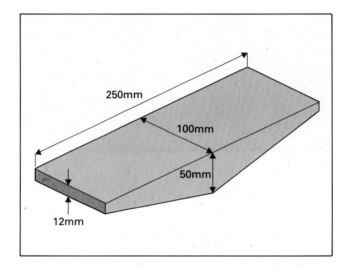

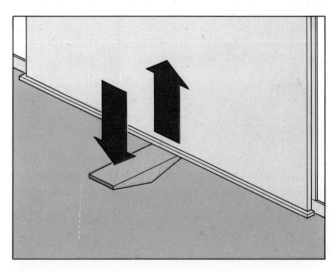

When fitting the plasterboard, you will find the job easier if you use a footlifter. Shape this as shown from a piece of 100 × 50 mm (4 × 2 in) softwood. Always protect the bottom of the board with a length of batten.

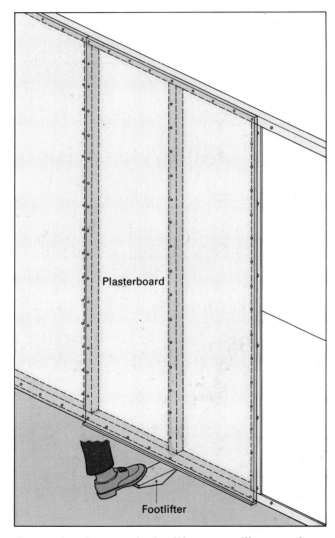

Plasterboard

Footlifter

By pressing down on the footlifter, you will ensure that the top edge of the plasterboard is tight against the ceiling. You can then nail it in place, taking care not to damage the paper covering when hammering.

When you come to fix the lengths of plasterboard to the batten framework, make sure you have the correct length galvanised clout nails and a hammer ready, since the boards are heavy and need to be supported as soon as possible. For the standard 12.5 mm ($\frac{1}{2}$ in) thick board, use 50 mm (2 in) nails; with 32 and 40 mm ($1\frac{1}{4}$ and $1\frac{1}{2}$ in) board use 65 mm ($2\frac{1}{2}$ in) nails; and with 50 mm (2 in) board, use 75 mm (3 in) nails.

To make the job of fitting easier, make up a footlifter (see diagram) to help press the board tight against the ceiling. With the board in the correct position, drive the nails in at 150 mm (6 in) intervals – and about 12 mm ($\frac{1}{2}$ in) in – round the edges. Drive the nails home until the head just dimples the surface of the board without breaking the paper covering.

You can tackle the window reveals in one of two ways. Either fit battens flush to the edges of each reveal, making sure there is a planed face on the outside to enable you to decorate it, or line the reveals with plasterboard as well (see diagram). In this case make sure that all exposed edges of plasterboard are bound ones. Any cut edges should be butted to the next section of board or put against the inside corners of the wall.

Finishing off Before you finish off the new wall, fix the skirting boards and door architraves back in place. Make sure the nails you use are long enough to fix into the battens by at least 20 mm ($\frac{3}{4}$ in). The bottom of the skirting boards must rest firmly on the floor and can be sealed with a non-setting mastic along their bottom edge. To conceal the join between the top of the new wall and the ceiling, you may like to fit coving. Full instructions are supplied when you buy the coving.

All electrical fittings will now have to be resited so that they are flush with the plasterboard surface. Normally there should be sufficient slack in the cable for you to pull it out from the wall to reach the new position of the fittings. If not, you will need to add

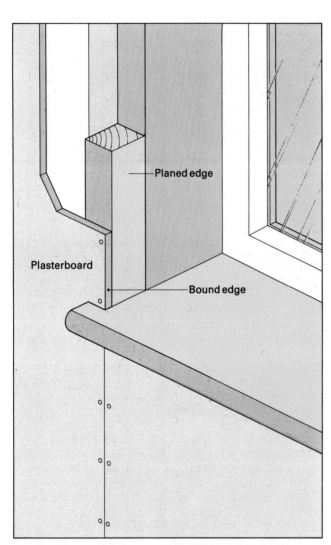

One method of tackling a window reveal is to run the framework and plasterboard flush to the edge. The bound edge of the board must be flush with the outer edge of the batten. Make good with plaster filler.

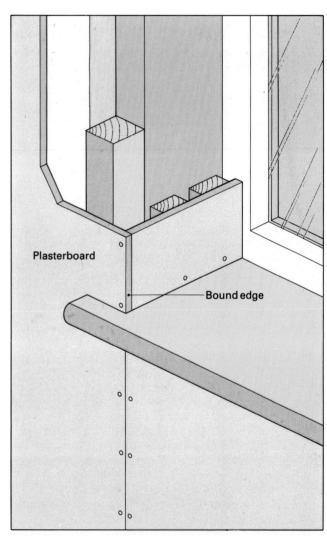

You will achieve slightly better insulation if you line the inside of the reveal as well. Ensure the raw edge of the plasterboard is against the window frame and make good any gaps with a plaster filler before redecorating.

short lengths of the same size and type of cable. To join the lengths of cable, use terminal connector strips and make sure that the conductors are paired up correctly – red (live) with red, black (neutral) with black and green/yellow (earth) with green/yellow.

If you had to move any radiators, you can now resite the brackets and hang the radiators. It is worth checking first what alterations are needed to the piping to and from these radiators, since you will want to make this job as easy as possible and it may be better to resite the radiators in a slightly different position. Having measured up where the brackets should go on the wall, screw these into battens behind the plasterboard. It is easiest to redecorate the wall before you finally hang the radiators in place.

To provide a neat finish to the plasterboard wall and enable you to redecorate successfully, you should fill in and finish off all joins between the boards. Here you will need joint filler, joint finish and joint tape and a 200 mm (8 in) jointing applicator, a 100 mm (4 in) taping or painter's knife and a sponge. You will notice that the plasterboards are tapered down their long edges. This is to enable you to make a flush joint.

First apply a continuous strip of joint filler into the tapered gaps. Then press suitable lengths of joint tape into this filler with the taping knife, working from the top down to make sure no air bubbles are left under the tape. Cover the tape with another coat of joint filler to provide a flush finish on all the joins and smooth down the edges with a moist sponge. Make sure you rinse out the sponge afterwards.

Leave the joins for about an hour and then apply a thin layer of joint finish. Again smooth down the edges with a moist sponge. When the first coat has dried, apply a second layer. Use joint filler over the nail heads and then apply some joint finish as well.

When the top layer of joint finish is dry, you can brush or roll on a special dry-wall top coat solution over the whole area of the new wall.

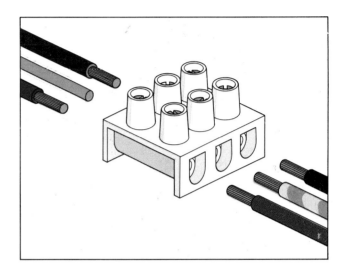

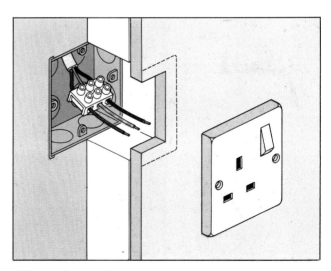

With sockets and switches, you may have to use connecting strip to extend the wiring. Connect up the conductors accurately. You may need longer screws or plasterboard fixing plugs to secure the switch plate.

Having fitted the lengths of plasterboard around the walls, you will need to make good all joints and gaps before decorating. Apply filler in the joints between each length and then press the joint tape into place. Cover this tape with another coat of joint filler, smoothing the surface with a painter's knife. When this has dried, apply joint finish along all the joins and rub down gently with a damp sponge to ensure a smooth surface.

Fixing thermal board

If the existing walls you want to insulate are in good condition – with a sound, flat and smooth surface – it is a lot quicker and easier to stick thermal board straight on to the wall. As already mentioned, this material is plasterboard with a polystyrene or polyurethane foam backing and should be handled and cut in the same way as ordinary plasterboard.

Thermal boards are available in sheets of 2400 × 1200 mm, 2440 × 1200 mm and 2700 × 1200 mm and in nominal thicknesses of 25, 32,

This thermal board is made up of 12.7 mm wallboard backed with a nominal 52.3 mm thickness of expanded polystyrene. The advantage of this type of board is that it has its own vapour barrier.

40, 50 and 65 mm (1, $1\frac{1}{4}$, $1\frac{1}{2}$, 2 and $2\frac{1}{2}$ in). Another significant advantage of this type of board is that because it incorporates its own vapour barrier, you do not need to fix polythene sheet underneath it.

To prepare the wall surface, remove skirting boards, door architraves and any electrical fittings, as before. Measure up on the wall for each length of board and cut this to fit from floor to ceiling. Make sure you cut out any holes to take existing wall fixtures and fittings before you secure the boards in place.

Mark the board widths along the wall and then apply the recommended adhesive to the wall in three vertical strips 200 mm (8 in) wide, one down each side and one down the middle, then horizontal strips along the top and bottom. Use a notched applicator, which is normally supplied with the adhesive. Hold each board in turn in position on the wall and tamp it firmly against the wall with a heavy timber straight-edge.

Having stuck the boards to the wall, secure them with special fixing plugs (see diagram). Drill suitable size holes through the boards into the wall. These should be made at the top, middle and bottom of each side of the boards and down the centre. The holes down the sides should be about 50 mm (2 in) in from the edges. When you make the holes, check they are deep enough so that the plugs penetrate the wall by about 32 mm ($1\frac{1}{4}$ in). Tap the plugs carefully into place until the countersunk heads are level or just fractionally below the surface of the boards. Insert the screws into each and tighten them until the head just dimples the surface.

The method you should use to tackle corners and reveals is explained in the diagrams. You should finish off the new wall, filling joins and providing a suitable surface for decorating, as you would with plasterboard (see above).

Note If the existing wall surface is not sound or even, you can still use thermal boards as insulation, but

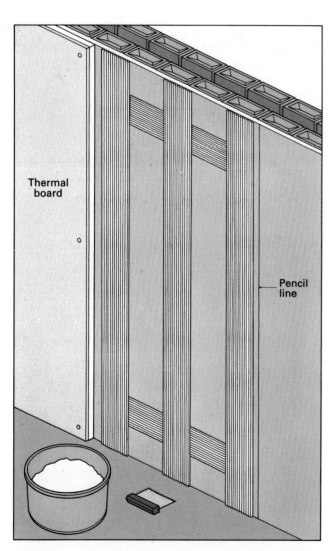

Thermal board

Pencil line

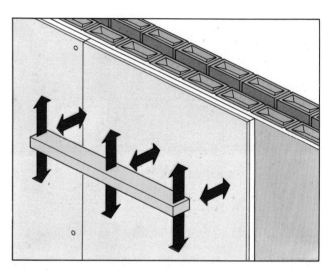

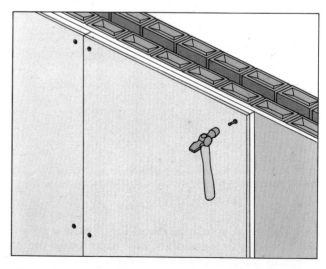

Provided that the walls are in good condition, you can fix thermal board straight on to them. Make sure the surface is dry and clean, then apply wide strips of adhesive. Work with one length of board at a time.

When you lay the thermal board on the adhesive, tamp it firmly into place with a long, heavy straight-edge, taking care not to damage the surface. Then secure it in place with special plugs, which take nails or screws.

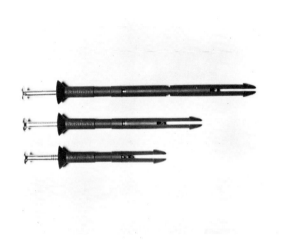

Special plugs are available to help secure thermal board to the walls. These must penetrate the wall by about 32 mm (I¼ in) and sit just below the surface of the board.

you will have to fit a timber batten framework 25 mm (I in) thick to the wall as already described (see above) and fix the thermal boards to it. Of course, you will not need to pack the cavity with any extra insulation material as you would with ordinary plasterboard.

Other insulating methods

Another way of insulating the inside of walls is by lining them with strips of tongued and grooved pine. If you fix the pine to a timber framework using battens 25 mm (I in) thick, this will enable you to fill the cavity created with 25 mm (I in) thick polystyrene or mineral fibre insulation in a similar way to that described above. Alternatively you can choose from a variety of coated hardboards. These are available in a range of grades and finishes, from simulated wood to melamine-coated decorative panels.

You can use lengths of expanded polystyrene and fix these to the walls in the same way as you would wallpaper. The polystyrene is available in rolls and normally comes in 5 mm (or ¼ in) thicknesses. Attach it to sound wall surfaces using a heavy duty wallpaper adhesive and then paper over it. These rolls are wider than rolls of wallpaper, so you do not have to worry about joins coinciding when you hang the wallpaper on top of the polystyrene.

There is now a type of wallpaper that incorporates a layer of aluminium foil to reflect back some of the heat in the room. Manufacturers claim this thermal wall covering has a high insulation value, but you should bear in mind that the insulation properties will be neutralised if you subsequently redecorate.

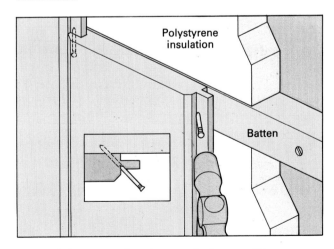

Polystyrene insulation

Batten

When fixing tongued and grooved pine panelling, you will need to use the secret nailing method as shown. Drive the head of the nail into the corner with a nail punch. This avoids unsightly nails showing.

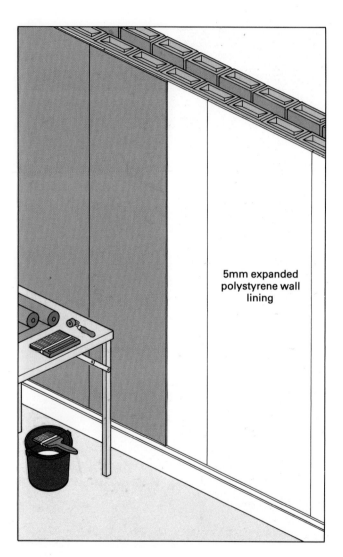

One way of providing extra insulation is to line the wall with lengths of polystyrene and then wallpaper over the top. When you hang the wallpaper, take care not to damage the surface of the polystyrene.

5mm expanded polystyrene wall lining

Insulating partition walls

In certain cases it may be worth considering insulating internal walls. This applies particularly where large areas in a house have been sub-divided into smaller rooms. A typical situation would be where a large house has been converted into several flats and rooms which have been created by fitting stud partition walls. These timber-framed double-skin walls contain a cavity between the two leaves. If this has not been insulated, a considerable amount of heat can be lost through the wall.

Unfortunately to insert insulation material into the cavity you will have to remove one side of the partition wall. If plasterboard has been used, you will find it very difficult to remove it intact, so you will have to budget to replace one side of the wall. Always take out the side of the wall that is in the warmer of the two adjoining rooms or areas, since the vapour barrier must be fitted on this side to check any moisture or condensation.

In this situation you can use rock or glass fibre or polystyrene panels as insulation, which should be cut to fit between the timber studs of the wall. You will need to fit polythene sheet over the whole wall as a vapour barrier (see page 50) before replacing the plasterboard sheets. Then seal off the joins and redecorate as already described.

Using radiator wall panels

You can buy aluminium-faced sheets to fit on to the wall behind radiators (see picture). The effect these have is to reflect back into the room the heat given off at the back of the radiator. Although it is difficult to estimate the exact efficiency of these sheets, they are comparatively inexpensive and therefore undoubtedly cost-effective. They are particularly useful behind radiators on external walls.

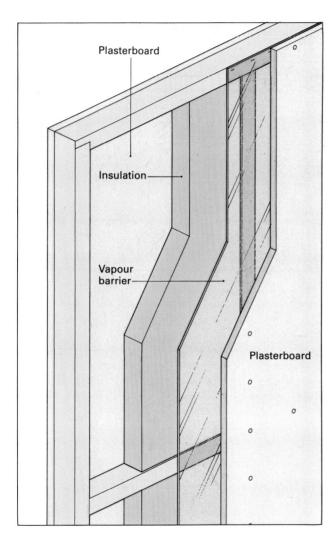

Plasterboard

Insulation

Vapour
barrier

Plasterboard

If you decide to insulate an internal partition wall, you must make sure that when you insert the polythene vapour barrier that this is fitted on the warmer side of the wall to prevent the formation of condensation.

Heat reflected panels, which you simply stick to the wall, throw the heat given off from behind radiators back into the room. Manufacturers claim that they can save up to 25% of the radiator heat.

4 The floors and ceilings

As much as 15% of the heat lost from the home is through the floors, although this will of course vary slightly, depending on the type of floors and the ventilation provided. The area where the greatest loss will occur is the ground floor, since it is with this floor that there is the greatest temperature difference either side.

The following U values for ground floors are typical of a medium-sized detached house. In a terraced house, you can virtually halve these figures.

The U value of a ventilated bare wooden floor on joists with airbricks on one side of the house only is 0.61. By covering the floor with linoleum, sheet vinyl or parquet flooring, the U value is reduced to 0.59. Where airbricks are fitted to more than one side of the house, the U value rises to 0.82 and 0.69 respectively. Where you have a solid floor laid on top of the ground with no cavity underneath, the U value is down to 0.56.

With intermediate floors, the U value will depend on which way the heat is flowing. For example, with a bedroom above a living room the heat loss will pass upwards from the living room. Assuming the floor to be of wood on joists with a plasterboard ceiling beneath, the U value is 1.7. If the situation is reversed and the heat loss is flowing down from the bedroom, the U value is 1.5.

Wooden ground floors

These floors are normally found in older properties, although you may have wooden floors fitted in some newer houses. You can fit insulation above them and, in most cases, below as well.

One important word of warning before you embark on any insulation. Do not be tempted to block off airbricks or ventilation ducts to keep the heat in. These have been fitted to ensure there is sufficient air passing underneath the wooden floor to prevent the formation of mould or rot.

Obviously it is a major job to lift a complete wooden floor to install insulation underneath. An ideal time to carry out this work is if you are lifting boards for some other reason – for example, to get at the wiring or plumbing system or to repair or replace loose or damaged boards.

The first job is to lift the floorboards. You should be able to do this without moving the skirting boards. If not, you will have to take these off the wall. The skirting boards are normally held in place on the wall by nails. To remove them you should use a bolster chisel or similar wide-bladed tool to ease them away from the wall. If you use a narrow-bladed tool, such as a screwdriver or normal wood chisel, you will damage the top edge of the boards.

Before you resite the skirting, smear non-setting mastic along the bottom edge to ensure a good seal between the boards and the floor. Remove the old nails and fix back the lengths of board with new masonry nails.

Lifting floorboards

Before you lift the floorboards, check the floor carefully to see whether any boards have been taken up before. The obvious clues to look for are new nails or screws or marks on the edges of the boards. These boards will be easier to lift than those that have never been disturbed.

You will also need to check on whether the boards are tongued and grooved. You can do this with a thin-bladed knife by sliding it between two boards; if it hits an obstruction, then the boards are

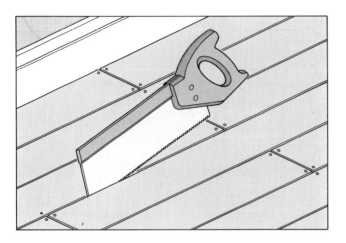

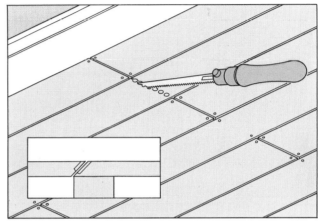

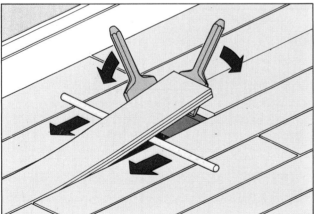

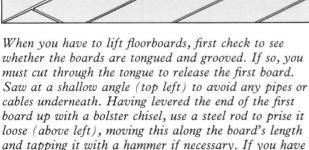

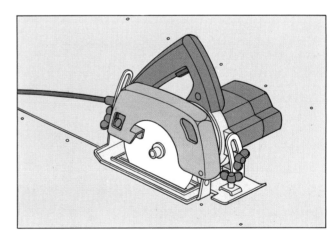

When you have to lift floorboards, first check to see whether the boards are tongued and grooved. If so, you must cut through the tongue to release the first board. Saw at a shallow angle (top left) to avoid any pipes or cables underneath. Having levered the end of the first board up with a bolster chisel, use a steel rod to prise it loose (above left), moving this along the board's length and tapping it with a hammer if necessary. If you have
to cut across the middle of a board, first drill a series of holes at an angle so that you can get in the blade of a padsaw. Then cut across the board at an angle (top right) so that you can fix through both parts of the board when you lay it back down. If you have flooring panels, these are best cut with a circular power saw (above right), set to the correct depth, above one of the joists to which they are fixed.

tongued and you will have to cut through the length of the tongues on adjoining boards in order to release it. The rest should then slide out after you have removed the nails or screws. Use a tenon saw to do this, but make sure you cut through the tongue at a shallow angle to prevent possible damage to any cables or pipes underneath.

Having selected the first board to lift, check on how it is fixed to the joists. If it is nailed down, you can pull these out as you lift the board. If, however, screws have been used, you should try to remove these first with a screwdriver. Dirt will have got into the holes and you will need to clean this off to locate the screws. You may have to ease them off with a little oil before removing them.

Ease the first board up with a bolster chisel. As soon as there is enough room, insert a long cold chisel or metal rod under the board and tap this along it, lifting as you go. You may need to use some extra force to get the end of the board clear of the wall, but be careful it does not spring up violently or damage the skirting board, if left in place.

If you cannot find a convenient end of board to lift, you will have to cut across one. Always cut above the centre of a joist, which you can locate by the position of the fixing nails or screws. Remove the screws or punch down the nails well below the surface, then drill a series of 3 mm ($\frac{1}{8}$ in) holes at an angle along the cutting line so that you can insert the blade of a padsaw. Make sure you cut through the board at an angle, so that you can screw through both cut ends of the board when you come to refix it.

When replacing the floorboards, use 50 mm (2 in) No 10 countersunk screws to fix each length back in place. With this type of fixing, you will find it a lot easier to lift the boards again, should this be necessary. Make sure you seal the gaps between the boards afterwards (see page 64).

If you have chipboard flooring panels, you should be able to insert blanket insulation by removing selective ones across the room. These panels are quite brittle and you will probably find you have to replace the ones you lift with new panels, because of damage.

To remove a panel, you should saw all round the edges to a depth of 20 mm ($\frac{3}{4}$ in) over the centre of the relevant joists. You can use a tenon saw as described above, but you will find it easier to use a circular power saw set to the correct depth. Having insulated the space underneath, fit the replacement panel with screws.

Always check on the condition of the joists underneath in case there are any signs of rot or woodworm. If there is any damage, then the affected parts must be cut out, burned and then replaced with treated timber. Even if the timbers are sound, it is a sensible precaution while you have access to treat them with a proprietary solution of wood preservative.

The ideal insulation material is the glass fibre

One effective method of insulating timber floors is to lay glass fibre blanket between the joists. To hold this in place you must staple or pin lengths of plastic netting, then lay lengths of glass fibre on top.

blanket used in the loft (see pages 28–30). You will, however, need to provide some support underneath and here you should staple or pin plastic netting to the underside of the joists, onto which you can put the glass fibre blanket. When you lay this between the joists, make sure that you leave a gap of at least 25 mm (1 in) between the top of the insulation and the underside of the floorboards. As an alternative you can use flanged building roll here (see below).

If, when you start lifting the floorboards, you find that there is a sufficiently large gap between the bottom of the joists and the concrete oversite beneath them to allow you to move around, you may be able to fit insulation from beneath. In this case, you will only have to lift enough floorboards to give you access to the space beneath.

In this situation, the best material to use is paper-faced, glass fibre building roll, which can be tacked or stapled to the joists. This material is available in two forms. One version is simple glass fibre insulation layered on either side with paper. The other is flanged either side of the insulation material, which is bonded to layers of Kraft paper that are wider than the glass fibre inside. You will need to work out exactly how many boards you need to lift to be able to feed the roll under the joists. The building roll type of insulation is, of course, also suitable should you have to lift up all the floorboards.

Lagging pipes While you have some or all of the floorboards up, this is a perfect opportunity to check the water pipes. Whether these supply the central heating or are just feed pipes to your taps, you should lag them. Make sure the lagging is at least 32 mm (or $1\frac{1}{4}$ in) thick.

You can either use glass fibre wrap or moulded sections of lagging, which clip over the pipes. In the latter case, make sure you buy the right size sections for the pipes to be lagged.

Despite arguments to the contrary, an unlagged hot water pipe is a very inefficient form of heating.

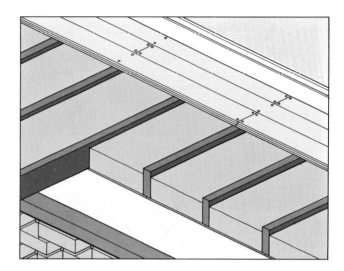

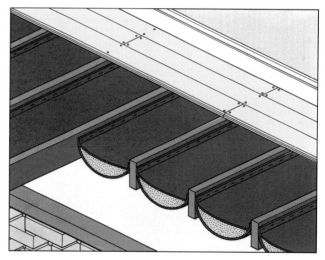

If you want to fit ordinary building roll under the floorboards (top), you should do this before the floor is laid. If the floor is already down you may be able to fix flanged building roll (above) if there is enough access.

Replacing floorboards   When you come to replace
the floorboards, if these are tongued and grooved
make sure that the lengths are correctly joined to
prevent draughts getting through. These joins can be
sealed up as additional protection (see below).

If you are fitting new floorboards, it is a sensible
precaution to store them indoors, preferably in the
same room in which they are to be fitted, for at least
two weeks before laying. This helps them to dry out
to the same moisture content as the room and avoids
the problem of boards shrinking and gaps appearing.

Having put back the flooring, refit the skirting
boards. Here it is also important to fill any gaps,
since otherwise draughts will get up through the ends
of the boards and under the skirting. One useful idea
is to apply non-setting mastic to the bottom edge of
all lengths of skirting before fitting them in place.
This will help provide a draughtproof seal between
the skirting and the top of the floorboards.

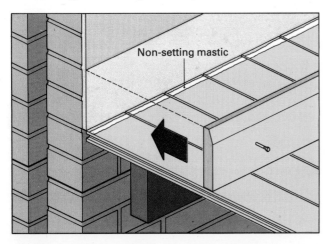

*When refitting the skirting boards, spread a layer of
non-setting mastic underneath before you fix them in
place. This will ensure a good seal between the bottom
edge and the floor to eliminate draughts.*

Insulating above the floor

If it proves impractical to insulate beneath the
flooring, there are various measures you can take to
insulate the floor from above. Check all the joins in
the flooring and seal up any gaps. This is best done
by using a non-setting mastic, which will cut out any
draughts but enable you to lift the flooring at a later
date if necessary. Alternatively you can use a plastic
wood filler.

One of the most effective forms of above-floor
insulation is a fitted carpet with a good quality felt
underlay. To improve the insulation of the floor even
further, you can lay special insulated flooring above
the existing floor (see Solid floors below).

Solid floors

There is no practical method of adding insulation
beneath an existing solid floor. If you happen to be
laying a new solid floor, then you can do this over an
insulating glass fibre blanket. But this job is outside
the scope of this book.

You can reduce the U value of an existing solid
floor quite considerably by laying chipboard sheets
over insulated flooring panels. These are made from
expanded polystyrene and are available with a
minimum thickness of 19 mm (or $\frac{3}{4}$ in). They come in
a standard size of 2440 × 1200 mm (8 × 4 ft).

Before you lay the new flooring, you must make
sure that the existing surface is dry, clean and level.
All the skirting will have to be removed as well.

Levelling the floor   Worn or uneven floors will
aggravate any problems you have from draughts. As
part of the remedy, you may have to level them off to
eliminate gaps under the skirting boards. Depending
on whether you have a suspended timber floor on a
solid concrete floor, there are two basic treatments.

In both cases you will need to remove the skirting

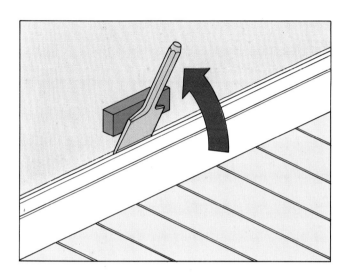

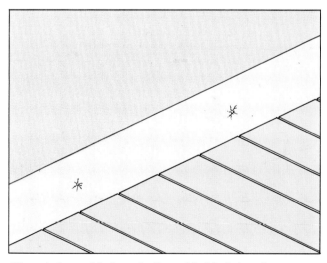

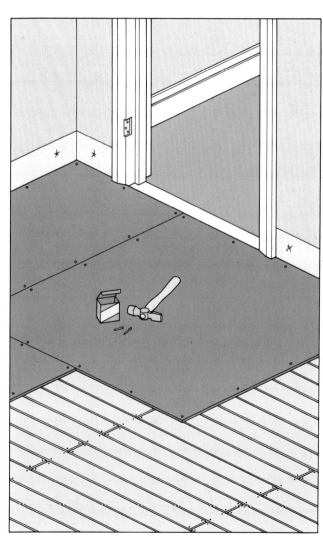

Use a bolster chisel or similar wide-bladed tool to ease the skirting board away from the wall, with a piece of wood packing to protect the plaster. Any damage caused behind the skirting board will be hidden when the board

is put back. Before you fix the sheets of tempered hardboard in place, you should soak them in water and let them dry out completely. This ensures that the boards will lie flat after fixing.

If you are insulating a solid floor, you must ensure the surface is smooth, level and sound. If there are any depressions, line them by brushing on a PVA screeding agent then fill with the correct mortar mix, smoothing

the surface with a float. Allow this to dry completely before laying a screed over the floor. Then spread the screeding compound across the whole floor, working from the farthest corner towards the door.

boards and all floor coverings. Then wash down the floor surface using a strong sugar soap solution, rinse with clean water and allow it to dry thoroughly. If any of the doors in the room open inwards, you must remove them by unscrewing the hinges.

To level off a timber floor you will have to lay down sheets of tempered hardboard. Make sure you wet them thoroughly first, so that they can dry flat when fitted. Position the sheets shiny side up, butt-joining them together to ensure there are no gaps. Fix the sheets in place using 20 mm ($\frac{3}{4}$ in) long panel pins or lost-head nails at 300 mm (12 in) intervals round the edges. Having fitted them to the floor, you can then refit the skirting boards, provided that no further insulation has to be fitted.

The easiest way to level off concrete floors is to use a self-levelling screeding compound. Check before you apply the screed that you fill any holes or depressions more than 6 mm ($\frac{1}{4}$ in) deep. Having washed down the floor and removed all dust and debris, coat any holes or depressions to be filled with a PVA bonding agent, diluted to the manufacturer's instructions. Then mix sufficient mortar – one part cement to three parts sharp sand – to fill them. Apply a second coat of PVA bonding agent and then the mortar before the agent dries. Level off the mortar with a float.

Mix the screeding compound with water in a bucket until you get a creamy paste. Starting at the furthest end of the room from the door, pour some of the screed on to the floor and smooth it into place with a float to a thickness of 2–3 mm ($\frac{1}{16}-\frac{1}{8}$ in). Continue this operation back across the room to the door. If you need another layer, you can apply more screed as soon as the first coat has dried – normally about two hours. Then leave it for 24 hours before refitting the skirting boards with masonry nails, provided that no futher insulation has to be fitted. Make sure the bottom edge of the boards rests on the new floor and use non-setting mastic on this edge if

you want to ensure a complete seal.

You may find you need to plane off a small amount from the bottom of any doors opening into the room to enable them to clear the new floor level (see below).

Laying the flooring Fit the insulated flooring panels so that the edges butt closely together and cover every part of the floor, including all awkward areas and corners. The panels can easily be cut to shape with a panel saw.

You need to cover these panels with a vapour barrier and for this you can use 100 gauge polythene sheet, which can be bought in 2 m (or 6 ft) strips. When fitting the polythene, overlap the joins by at least 75 mm (3 in). You can hold the strips in place with small pieces of self-adhesive PVC tape.

The sheets of chipboard can now be laid on top of the floor insulation. Measure up and work out a plan for these to keep any cutting of sheets to a minimum. Make sure when you do this that the joins between sheets do not coincide with the joins between the polystyrene panels underneath.

Secure the edges of the chipboard to adjoining sheets with contact adhesive, but leave a gap of 10–12 mm (or about $\frac{1}{2}$ in) all round the edge of the room between the chipboard and the walls to allow for expansion. Replace the skirting board so that the bottom edge of each length rests on the chipboard and thus hides the expansion gap.

Refitting a door Stand the door in its frame and position it so it is nearly closed. Use scrap pieces of card underneath to lift it just clear of the floor. Fold the hinges against the existing recesses and measure how much higher the hinges are than the top of the recesses. This amount needs to be trimmed off the bottom of the door. You can plane small amounts off the door, but if you have to remove more than 3 mm ($\frac{1}{8}$ in), use a fine-toothed saw. Do not forget to make allowance for any floor covering you will be laying down afterwards. You may also want to fit some form

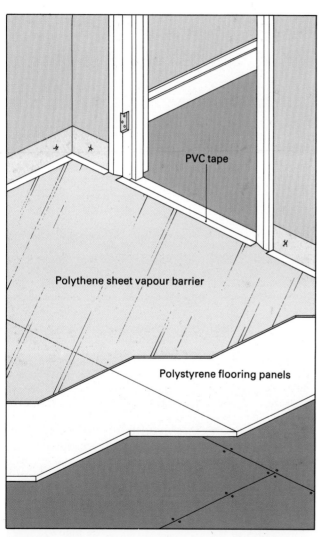

PVC tape

Polythene sheet vapour barrier

Polystyrene flooring panels

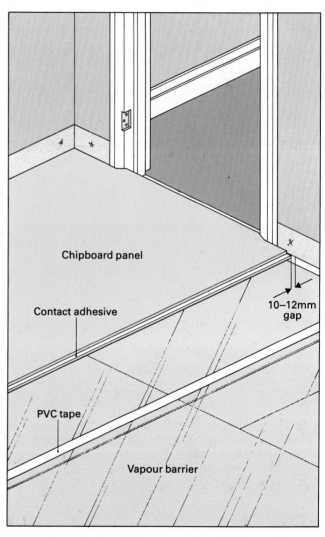

Chipboard panel

Contact adhesive

10–12mm gap

PVC tape

Vapour barrier

When the floor surface is sound, lay the polystyrene flooring panels, making sure there are no gaps between them. You can then put down the polythene vapour barrier, sealing any joints with PVC tape. Check there are no tears in it and if necessary patch these with tape as well. When you fit the chipboard panels, fix the joining edges with a contact adhesive. Leave a gap of 10 mm (or ½ in) round the room for expansion.

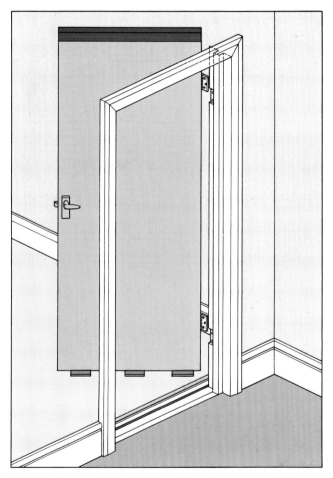

Having increased the height of the floor, you will have to trim the bottom of any door opening inwards. Hold the door against the frame and measure how much it overlaps at the top (shaded section). This is the amount to trim from the bottom.

of draught excluder at the bottom of the door as well (see page 91).

You can get insulated panels in other materials. The basic method of installation will be the same as that described here, but you should always check the manufacturer's instructions for specific recommendations.

Intermediate floors

The amount of heat lost through these floors is relatively insignificant if the house is fully centrally heated. If, however, you are heating a living room downstairs and the room above is not heated at all, then you can reduce the cost of heating the downstairs room by insulating the intermediate floor. This, of course, would mean that the room upstairs would be even colder.

While it would be an advantage to save wasting heat and maintaining a temperature of around 15–18°C in an upstairs room that is not being used, you will have to decide whether the cost of insulating the floor is really justified in terms of the amount of heat saved. You will have to consider each case on its own merit before deciding to spend a considerable amount of money on insulation. This means checking on the U value of the flooring and taking into account the temperature differences between the two rooms in question.

The simplest and one of the cheaper ways of effecting some insulation is to fit a thick pile carpet with a good quality felt underlay in the upstairs room. You can augment this by fitting insulating ceiling tiles in the downstairs room (see below).

Another, more effective but costly method is to fit insulated flooring panels in the upstairs room, using the method described for solid floors. Bear in mind that this will raise the floor level by about 50 mm

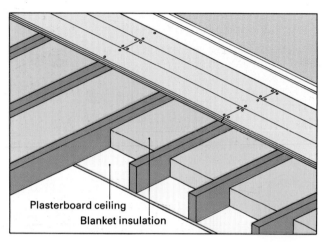

If you want to lay blanket insulation under intermediate floors, you will have to lift some of the floorboards. As you feed in the insulation, check that you do not interfere with any wiring and leave a ventilation gap.

Plasterboard ceiling
Blanket insulation

(2 in), so you will need to fit a threshold where any door in that room leads out to another area. Equally you will need to trim off the bottom of any door that opens inwards.

If you suffer from a noise problem in an upstairs room, it is worth considering using panels with impact sound insulation. These considerably reduce the transmission of unwanted noise, either from above or below.

A very effective method of insulating intermediate floors, but one that involves the most work, is to install blanket insulation between the plasterboard ceiling and the floorboards above. If you decide to install this type of insulation, you must make sure that when laid there is still a gap of 25 mm (1 in) between the top of the insulation and the floorboards above. You will have to lift most of the floorboards in order to gain access to the gap between each of the floor joists (see pages 60–62).

When laying insulation under the floor, take care not to damage or interfere with existing cable or pipe runs. Ideally electric cables should lie above the insulation so that any heat generated by the flow of electricity through them can be dissipated. Again, if you are lifting floorboards, you will have the opportunity of lagging any water pipes under the floorboards (see page 63). Check that you are not wasting money by lagging gas pipes in mistake for water pipes.

Bear in mind if you do lay insulation in intermediate floors, that the heat loss gained from the rooms below will mean colder rooms above, unless these are centrally heated anyway. This will, of course, further reduce heat loss through the roof.

Ceilings

By insulating the ceiling of a room, you will not only retain more heat within that room but you may also be able to add to the aesthetic value of that area. This may well be the case in older houses with lofty ceilings, where to increase the insulation you can install a suspended ceiling which will reduce the volume of that room and therefore the cost of heating it. If, however, you decide to lower the ceiling, you should maintain a minimum height of 2.3 m (7 ft 6 in) from the floor.

Fitting a false ceiling

There are two basic methods of fitting a false ceiling. One involves making a strong timber framework on to which you can fix sheets of plasterboard or thermal board. Alternatively you can fit a lightweight framework of aluminium T-section, suspended from the existing ceiling, and insert insulating tiles into it.
Timber framework Having decided on the height

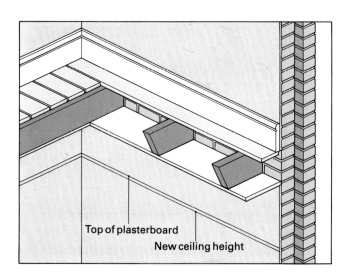

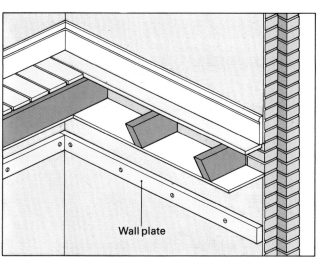

Top of plasterboard
New ceiling height

Wall plate

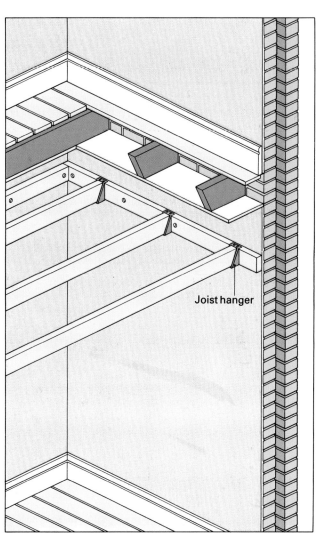

Joist hanger

When marking round the top of the walls to fit a
suspended timber ceiling, the top line should indicate the
top of the plasterboard and the bottom line the level of
the new ceiling. As you fit the wall plates round the

walls, the bottom edge of these lengths must be flush with
the top marked line. The next stage is to fit joists across
the room, from which to support the new ceiling. Fix
these to the wall plates with steel joist hangers.

71

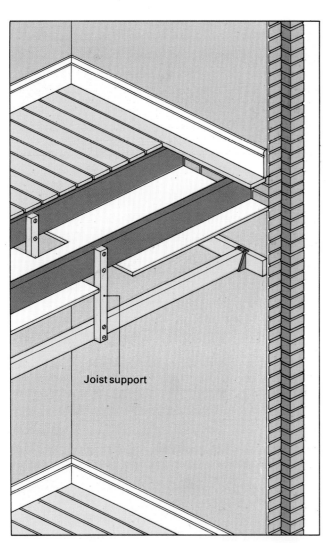

Joist support

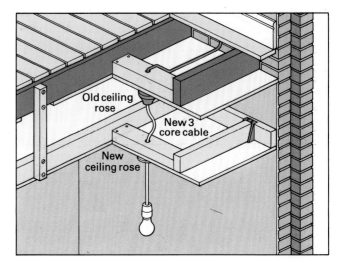

Old ceiling rose

New 3 core cable

New ceiling rose

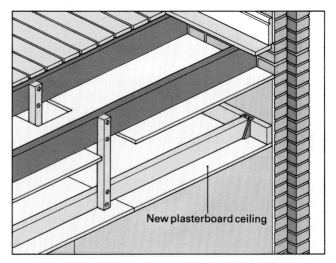

New plasterboard ceiling

If the room is more than 2.5 m (or 8 ft) wide, you will need to support the joists for the new ceiling to prevent it from sagging. Screw suitable length pieces of timber between the original and the new joists. Then remount any light fittings with a new ceiling rose fixed to the new ceiling. Finally fix sheets of plasterboard to the new joists with galvanised nails, make good any gaps or joins between sheets (see pages 53–54) and redecorate.

of the new ceiling, mark a line all round the walls using a spirit level and long straight-edge to make sure the line is horizontal. Then mark a second line the same distance above this line as the thickness of the plasterboard or thermal board you are using. This line corresponds to the bottom of the fixing joists.

Measure up the lengths of joist required for the new ceiling, bearing in mind that the joists should run across the shortest distance between opposite walls – that is, the width rather than the length. Unless the room is small, you will need to support these joists from the ceiling. The smallest size joist you should use is 100 × 50 mm (4 × 2 in) and the timber must be straight-grained and properly seasoned. You can save money by buying sawn wood and not planed, but it must be good quality.

The joists will span up to 2.5 m (or 8 ft) without any central support. If your room is wider than this, you will have to support the middle of each joist with another piece of timber fixed to the original ceiling joist (see diagram).

Before you fit the joists across the room you will have to fix lengths of timber the same thickness as the joists all round the room, so their bottom edge is on the higher of the two marked lines on the walls. These timbers are called wall plates. You must fix these very securely since they will carry most, if not all, of the weight of the ceiling. Use 100 mm (4 in) No 12 countersunk screws at 450 mm (18 in) intervals, drilling holes in the timber first and then marking the fixing points through the holes on to the walls. Drill and plug holes in the walls and then screw on the timbers.

You can now fit the joists across the room. This should be done by using metal joist hangers fixed to the wall plates at 600 mm (2 ft) intervals (see diagram). If necessary, you will now have to fit supports at the middle of each joist to the original ceiling joists using 50 × 50 mm (2 × 2 in) timber.

Having installed the timber framework, you can fix on the plasterboard or thermal board to the underside (see pages 50–57). Before you do this, however, you must remember to move down any ceiling light fittings. First switch off at the mains, then remove the cover of the light fitting. With a suitable length of three-core cable the same size as that in the fitting, connect up the conductors to the terminals in the fitting – live (red) to live, neutral (black) to neutral and earth (green/yellow) to earth.

You will probably have to make a small timber framework between the new joists on which to mount the new fitting (see diagram). Having fitted on the boards and made a hole where the cable comes, mount the new light fitting and connect up the free end of cable to the relevant terminals (see above).

Aluminium framework You will find a lightweight aluminium frame easier to fit than a timber one and kits are available which, when fitted, will take insulating tiles or illuminated panels to complete the new ceiling.

Having marked all round the walls the line of the new ceiling as described above, fix the edge support sections round the walls, having first drilled and plugged holes at the correct intervals to take the fixing screws. You can now fix the main support tees according to the manufacturer's instructions. Normally these are spaced 600 mm (2 ft) apart. Any odd dimensions can be made up either at one side of the room or in equal amounts at each side. If you have to support long lengths of these tees, you can usually do this by screwing large hooks into the original ceiling joists and holding the tees with lengths of wire fitted to the hooks.

The bridging tees should be fitted next. The method used will vary depending on the manufacturer and you should check with the instructions first. Again you can make up odd dimensions at one side or equal amounts at each side of the room. Finally put the tiles in place. You will

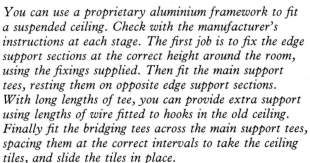

You can use a proprietary aluminium framework to fit a suspended ceiling. Check with the manufacturer's instructions at each stage. The first job is to fix the edge support sections at the correct height around the room, using the fixings supplied. Then fit the main support tees, resting them on opposite edge support sections. With long lengths of tee, you can provide extra support using lengths of wire fitted to hooks in the old ceiling. Finally fit the bridging tees across the main support tees, spacing them at the correct intervals to take the ceiling tiles, and slide the tiles in place.

have to slide them diagonally through the framework and then lower them on to the aluminium sections. If you have any odd size holes, you can easily cut the tiles to shape with a sharp cutting knife.

Lining a ceiling

The cheapest and easiest way of improving the insulation qualities of a ceiling is to fit ceiling tiles or panels, which are now available in a large variety of styles and patterns. Apart from combatting heat loss, some have sound-reducing properties, which are particularly useful if you are living in a downstairs flat or want to isolate the noise of a living room from a bedroom above.

The materials from which these tiles or panels are made vary considerably, from expanded polystyrene to rock fibres. Always check with the manufacturer as to the type of adhesive recommended for fitting. It is particularly important with polystyrene tiles that you use the correct adhesive and that you cover the whole area of the back of the tile with adhesive. The original method of applying a blob of mastic-type adhesive in each corner and in the centre of a tile has been recognised as a fire hazard, since the air retained under the tiles aids combustion.

When you buy any polystyrene material for this purpose, check that it has a flame-retardant (formerly known as self-extinguishing) additive in it.

Before you fit tiles to the ceiling, you must locate the centre point on the ceiling. To do this, measure and mark the midway point along each of the four walls. Pin two lengths of string across the ceiling, one across the width and the other along the length. Where these lengths cross will be the centre. Mark this point on the ceiling and along the string in each direction for about 300 mm (1 ft). This will enable you to line up the first four tiles correctly.

Using the recommended tile adhesive, brush it liberally on to the back of each tile. Position the first tile immediately on the ceiling and press it firmly in place for about 20 seconds, using a piece of hardboard or plywood cut to approximately the size of the tile. This will prevent the possibility of damage to the tile from finger pressure. Fit the other three central tiles in the same way, butting the edges of each tight against the adjoining tile. Continue tiling the rest of the ceiling with full tiles.

To measure up the border tiles, hold a full tile on top of the last fixed tile in each row in turn. Place another tile over this one but with its edge butting up to the wall. Mark with a pencil along the edge of this tile furthest from the wall on to the tile beneath. Cut the marked tile along this line to give you the exact shape of the border tile. To do this you should use either a hot wire cutter or a wet cutting knife against a metal straight-edge. Repeat this procedure for each border tile around the room.

For a neat finish, you can fix polystyrene coving in the angle of the walls and ceiling. This is supplied in 1 or 2 m (3 ft 3 in or 6 ft 6 in) lengths and internal and external corner pieces are available. You stick it in position using the same adhesive as the tiles (see diagram). If you decide to paint the coving – or the tiles – you should use emulsion or a fire-retardant finish. Never use gloss paint since it creates a fire hazard in this situation.

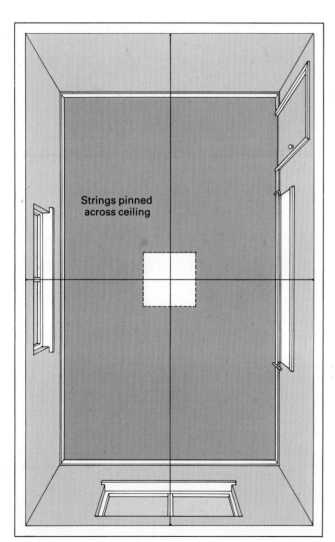

Ceiling tiles should be fitted from the centre of the room outwards to the walls. To establish the centre point, pin lengths of string between the centres of opposite pairs of walls. Where they cross is the centre of the room.

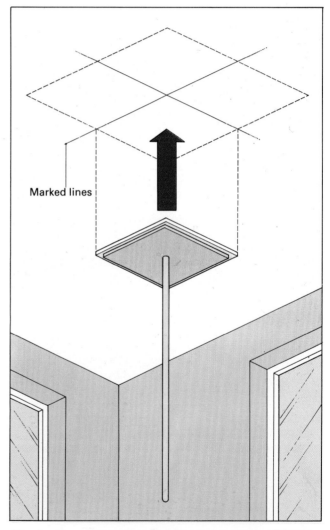

Fix the first tile in place with the recommended adhesive so that one corner coincides with the centre point of the ceiling. To avoid damage to the tiles, use a square of plywood on the end of a pole to secure each tile in place.

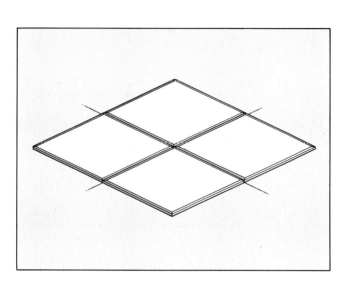

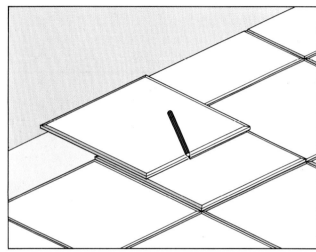

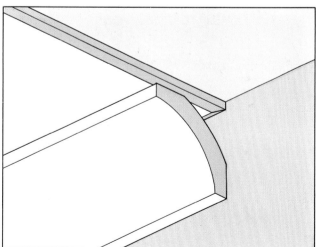

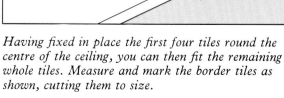

Having fixed in place the first four tiles round the centre of the ceiling, you can then fit the remaining whole tiles. Measure and mark the border tiles as shown, cutting them to size.

Coving provides a neat finish to the wall-ceiling joint around the room and is fixed in place with recommended adhesive on the wall and ceiling. Corners should be mitred using the gauge provided to ensure the best effect.

5 Draughts

It has been estimated that if all draughts in the average house were put together they would represent a hole a metre square on the outside wall. Although it is impossible to give an accurate figure, it is reasonable to assume that approximately 15% of heat lost from a house is through draughts.

Draughts are caused by two basic factors. Hot air which rises due to convection, escapes up chimneys, through doors and any other gaps it can find. This causes cold air to be drawn into the room to replace the hot air. Windy conditions outside the house cause a pressure difference between the outside and the inside. This in turn results in cold air finding its way through cracks or openings in external door and window frames, for example.

Ventilation

From the above it may appear that the solution to draught problems is to seal up all openings both inside and outside the house to prevent any movement of air through the house. Unfortunately this is neither practical nor advisable since all rooms need their air to be changed at various times through the day. This is necessary for the following reasons:
- to ensure there is an adequate supply of oxygen necessary for breathing
- to remove the carbon dioxide and water vapour breathed out or given off by flames
- to remove stale air and odours (this is important in bathrooms and kitchens)
- to prevent the formation of mould due to a static high humidity level

Air changes Assuming wintry conditions, with a temperature of -1°C, living rooms with a temperature of 21°C need 1–1½ air changes per hour.

The type of conditions that will affect individual rooms include, for example, the use of a shower in the bathroom, which will increase the humidity level and therefore demand more frequent air changes. In such a situation, an extractor fan may be necessary.

Effects from heating appliances

Draughts caused when you use electric fires and convector heaters are minimal and in most cases would go unnoticed since they are only created by whatever hot air might escape high up in the room. With an open solid fuel or gas fire that uses a conventional chimney to take away the fumes caused by the combustion, the air that goes up the chimney has to be replaced and here draughts are much more evident.

Some flow of air is essential where solid fuel or gas is being burned, since the fumes given off can be quite dangerous, particularly those from a gas fire. Equally an open fire will smoke if no replacement air is available and the smoke will work its way through the room. Under these circumstances you must allow some air into the room.

The most satisfactory way of doing this and keeping draughts to a minimum is to provide a supply of air near the fire itself. You can do this by fitting an air vent connected to the underfloor space either in the floor or in the skirting board adjacent to the fire.

Fitting air vents If you are working with a suspended timber floor, you can fit a ventilation grille into the floor or skirting board adjacent to the fireplace. Obviously, having fitted the grille into the floor, you must make sure you do not then put a floor covering over it.

To fit a grille into the floor, you will need to drill a number of fairly large holes – about 20–25 mm

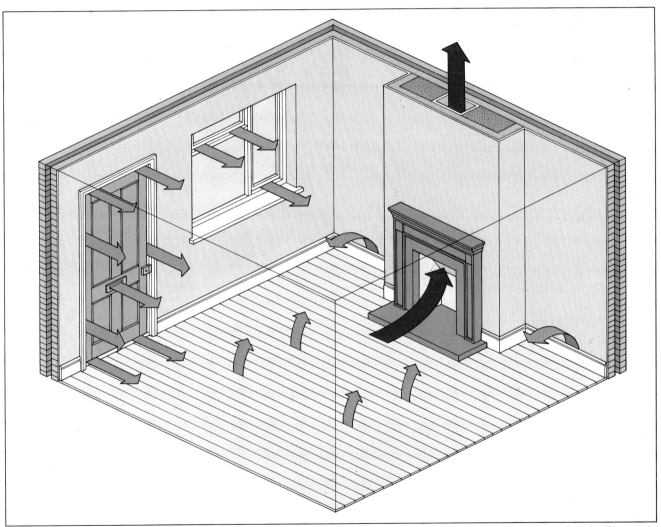

This diagram shows you the permutation of routes that draughts can take into a typical room, with the main exit provided by the chimney through an open fire. While steps should be taken to eliminate draughts as far as possible, it is equally important not to seal off a room completely. Some ventilation is required to facilitate air changes, depending on the use of the room, to prevent condensation and to remove the effects of stale air. It is also essential in those rooms where a solid fuel or gas fire is being used.

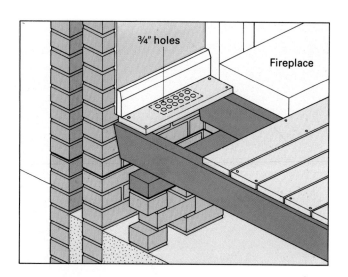

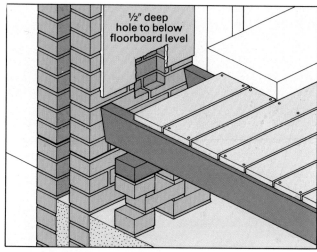

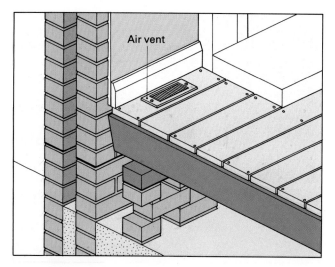

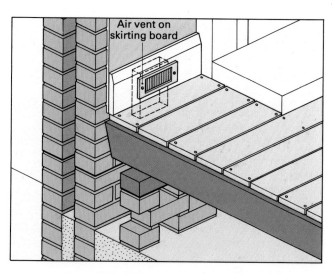

The simplest method of installing a vent is by fitting a grille in the floor, provided that it is of timber, having first drilled a series of holes in the floorboard. Position the vent between joists and leave it uncovered.

Another method involves fitting the grille to the bottom of the wall or skirting board. You will have to make a small channel in the brickwork. The advantage of this method is that it does not affect floor coverings.

($\frac{3}{4}$–1 in) in diameter – through the relevant section of floorboard. Make sure that you do not site the grille over a joist, the line of which should be quite easily located by the nails or screws used to fix down the boards into the joists. You can then fit the grille plate over the top of these holes. Usually it is held in place with screws.

Fitting a grille in the skirting is a little more complicated. First buy the grille and check if the skirting board is deep enough to accommodate it. If not, you will either have to fit deeper skirting board or install the grille in a gap in the skirting board.

In either case, decide on the position for the grille and mark it on the floor with pencil or masking tape. Remove the relevant section of skirting board and mark out the shape of the grille opening. This will be slightly smaller than the grille itself. Now drill a series of holes about 35 mm (or 1$\frac{1}{2}$ in) deep all round the edge of the marked area. You can remove the brickwork in the drilled area with a bolster chisel and hammer.

You will now have to extend this hole downward until it is approximately 25 mm (1 in) below the level of the floorboards. You can do this using the same drill and chisel technique as before.

If you are fitting the grille to the skirting board, you will have to cut a hole the same size as the grille opening in the skirting board. You can do this by drilling a series of holes with a 12 mm ($\frac{1}{2}$ in) drill bit and then cutting out the section with a padsaw. Refit the skirting board and fix the grille plate in position with the necessary screws.

If the grille is to be fitted to the wall, mark the grille plate screw positions on the wall and drill and plug these holes. Screw the grille plate in position, making good any damage to the surrounding area with a plaster filler. Now cut the skirting board and refit it round the grille.

If you have to stand any solid piece of furniture in front of this grille, make sure you leave a gap of

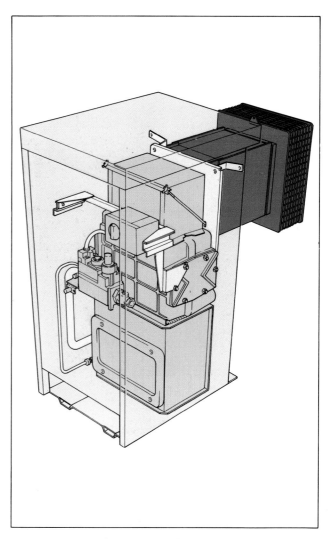

The advantage of a balanced flue gas fire or boiler is that the air for combustion is drawn from the outside and the waste products emitted back again. The flue, which must pass through an external wall, is shaded red.

about 50–75 mm (2–3 in), otherwise the effect of the grille in providing ventilation will be drastically reduced.

With a gas fire it is possible to have a balanced flue fitted where the fire is on an outside wall. With this type of arrangement the air necessary for combustion is drawn in from outside the building and the waste products from the combustion are emitted through the same flue. If you are thinking of fitting a balanced flue, you should first consult your local gas board.

False draughts from windows

Windows are notorious for letting in draughts. But the cause is not necessarily a badly fitting frame. With a single glazed window on a cold day the inside of the glass gets very cold and can be affected by condensation as the warm air inside comes into contact with it. As the air cools it falls down to the bottom of the window over the internal sill, below the curtains if drawn across and back into the room as a cold 'draught'.

No amount of sealing up of the window frame will prevent this 'draught' and the only complete solution to the problem is to install some form of double glazing (see Chapter 6). One way of reducing the effect of this draught, however, is to hang thick curtains that are long enough to start above the window opening and finish well below the sill.

How to trace draughts

This may sound unnecessary since draughts are easy enough to feel. But quite often it is difficult to find from where exactly a draught is coming. There are several simple ways of locating the source of a draught apart from 'dropping a feather'.

The simplest, safest and quickest method is to wet the tip of your finger and hold it up against any suspected gap. If the draught is blowing at that spot, your finger will feel cold – and the stronger the draught, the colder it will feel.

One traditional method is a lighted candle, where you simply watch for the flame to flicker or, in extreme cases, be blown out. A candle will detect the smallest draught, but it is not always safe or practical. You should never, for example, use it near inflammable material such as a curtain or drape and it cannot of course be used around the bottom of doors.

One tell-tale sign to look out for on window and door frames is a dirty patch on or around the inside corners of a frame. This may well have been caused by deposits of dirt and dust brought in by a draught from the outside.

Keeping out draughts

There are various ways in which this can be achieved. Your choice of prevention and cure will depend on the location and size of the problem and, of course, how much you are prepared to spend. The options available range from the cheapest and simplest method of fitting strips of insulation around the frames of doors and windows to the most permanent and effective method – installing double glazing (see Chapter 6).

Fitting insulation strip Different types of insulation strip are available, depending on your budget and the nature of the draught. The cheapest is self-adhesive PVC foam strip, which works quite well in sealing smallish gaps around doors and windows. It does, however, collect dirt easily, absorbs water and will after a while begin to look tatty. For these reasons it needs to be replaced every year or so.

Three different types of insulation strip, all with self-adhesive backing – (from left) foam, two rubber styles and atomic plastic. All these strips are suitable for use on doors and windows.

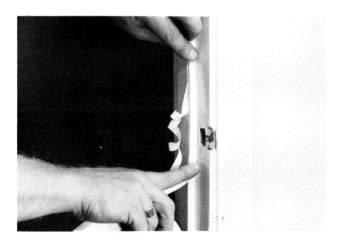

When fitting foam insulation strip, peel off the backing bit by bit as you press the strip into position on the closing edge of the frame.

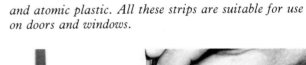
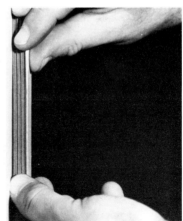

The rubber strip is fixed in a similar way to foam. Peel off the backing tape as you work round the frame. This type lasts longer and stays cleaner than foam strip.

The advantage of using plastic atomic strip is that the spring-loaded, non-fixing edge presses firmly against the door or window frame as it is closed.

Another type of strip that offers a longer life is made from high quality rubber and will seal gaps of 2–3 mm (about $\frac{1}{8}$ in). It is also self-adhesive and carries a five-year guarantee.

The oldest type of insulation strip consisting of a rubber tube with a flange fixing is still available and is now made from silicone rubber. You can fix it round frames using staples or pins or with silicone adhesive. It will insulate gaps of 3–5 mm ($\frac{1}{8}$–$\frac{1}{4}$ in).

A further form of draughtproofing is known as atomic strip. Available as either bronze or plastic strip, it has a wide wing and narrow edge, the latter being used to fix it to the door frame. When the strip is pinned down tightly, the wide wing presses against the edge of the door when closed. This strip is very simple to fit, but you should check that the wide wing does not foul the back of the frame when it is forced to spring back as the door is closed.

One of the more recent variations of insulation strip incorporates a brush pile seal. It looks like a continuous length of short-haired brush and is particularly suitable for sash windows and sliding doors.

The various types of insulation strip mentioned here involve different methods of fixing (see pictures).

Checking draughts through windows

The more recent aluminium window frames usually incorporate polypropylene, brush-type draught excluders, which should give long service. These can be replaced quite simply when they wear down by pulling out the old seals and sliding in the new ones.

The older galvanised steel and wooden framed casement windows are not normally fitted with any draught prevention devices and these are frequently the greatest sources of draughts in a room. The most effective way of stopping all draughts through these frames is by fitting well-made secondary windows (see Chapter 6). These will not only eliminate draughts through the frame but will also dramatically reduce the false draught you would normally get from a single glazed window.

If you decide not to fix secondary glazing, then you will have to deal with each source of draughts individually. Your treatment will depend on whether you are working on a casement, sash or louvre window.

Casement window First close each casement window in turn and check both from the inside and the outside to see whether any gaps of more than a millimetre are visible between the opening and fixed frames. If you find any gaps, you should fill them before carrying out any other preventative measures on that window.

Open the window again and clean all round the opening and fixed frames with a strong detergent or

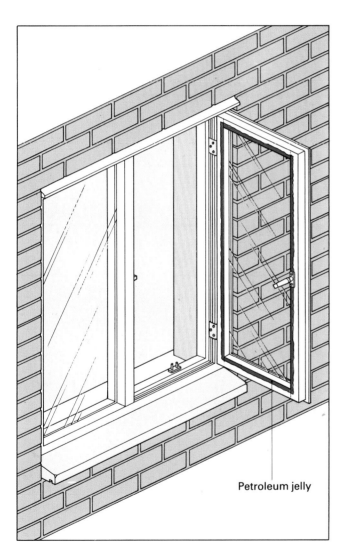

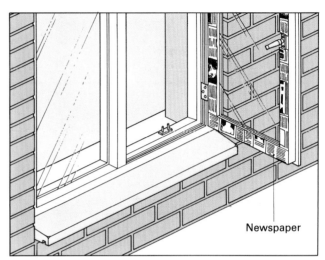

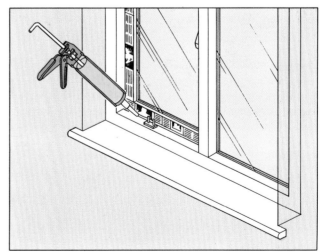

Petroleum jelly

Newspaper

This method of frame repair is best suited for old windows that may have larger, irregular gaps around the frames. Having washed and dried round the frames, smear petroleum jelly on the closing surfaces of the

opening frame. Then lay strips of newspaper over the jelly and close the window. Where gaps are visible, fill these with a setting mastic or filler and leave to set. Finally remove the newspaper and clean off the jelly.

white spirit. Dry the frames thoroughly and smear petroleum jelly on all the closing surfaces of the opening frame only.

Next stick strips of newspaper over the petroleum jelly, smoothing them in place with your fingers. Ensure that the strips are wide enough to give you at least a 25 mm (1 in) overlap on the fixed frame and then close the window again.

Fill the gap between the newspaper and fixed frame with a setting type of mastic, exterior grade plastic filler or two-pack resin filler. Allow this to set according to the manufacturer's instructions, then open the window and remove the strips of newspaper and wipe off the petroleum jelly.

If necessary, rub the new surface smooth with flour grade glasspaper, before applying undercoat and gloss paint to match the existing paint scheme.

Any smaller gaps remaining after this treatment can be filled using one of the range of draught insulation strips. Fit one length at a time, checking after each application to make sure that the window still shuts properly. Once you are satisfied you have filled up all the gaps between the frames, check that any window locks that are fitted still work properly.

Sash window This type of window presents a different problem. The most common source of draughts is the gap between the top and bottom frames when they are both closed. You will not normally get excessive draughts around the sides of a sash window, particularly with older ones which will usually have a lot more paint on them and therefore fit more tightly.

The best way of keeping out draughts from the gap between the two frames is to fit the brush-type strip (see page 84) on the meeting surface – that is at the bottom of the top frame and the top of the bottom frame.

This strip can also be fitted to the top of the top frame and the bottom of the bottom frame to eliminate any draughts around the top and bottom of the window when both halves are closed.

Louvre window Although the more expensive makes of louvre windows have built-in draught protection, some of the cheaper types rely on the close fit of each glass pane on to the adjoining one. Unfortunately the alignment of these panes is not always perfect and draughts will find a way through.

One way of cutting out the draughts is to apply insulation strip along the offending panes. But before you do this you should try to adjust the alignment, where it is out, to get the panes to fit properly. To do this you may have to resite the fixing screws of the pane supports or gently bend the metal supports. Any gaps that remain can be sealed with a suitable insulation strip.

A more effective, but unsightly, method to cure the problem in winter is to seal the panes closed with clear self-adhesive or masking tape. But in the end the only really practical way of sealing off any

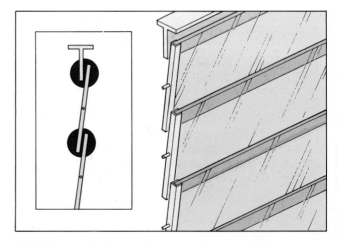

With louvred windows, it is sometimes possible to seal gaps where the panes meet by carefully altering the end frames on the louvres. Mechanisms do vary, however, depending on the manufacturer.

draughts, particularly with the cheaper louvre windows, is by fitting a secondary window inside (see Chapter 6).

Sealing other gaps round windows

There is one other area that can be the source of draughts and that is round the outside edge of the fixed window frame and under the sill. So check to see whether there are any gaps between the fixed frame and the wall and fill any you find with a non-setting mastic. This will ensure that the gap remains sealed even when the window frame expands and contracts within the opening in the brickwork due to changes in temperature, humidity and so on.

Curing draughts through internal doors

The main problem areas round an internal door are the bottom and side edges. You can normally ignore any draught through the top edge since this is unlikely to cause any discomfort in the room and also helps to ventilate it. Obviously a gaping hole at the top will have to be tackled.

First check that the door closes properly. If when you close it there is a uniform gap between the closing face of the door and the closing edge of the door frame, pull the door tightly shut to check whether this eliminates the gap. If it does, and the lock is in good condition, you may be able to adjust the position of the lock's striker plate to take up the gap.

Measure the width of the gap, then unscrew the striker plate from the door frame and reposition it by that amount nearer to the closing edge of the frame.

With a pencil, mark the new position of the striker plate and, if necesssary, chisel out a new seating recess for it. Holding the striker plate in its new position, mark the new screw holes with a bradawl and screw the striker plate in position. Fill any exposed part of the old recess with plastic wood or by gluing and pinning a suitable sized strip of wood in it.

Next check the gap between the edge of the door and the frame. This should be about 3 mm ($\frac{1}{8}$ in) to allow the door to close properly. If the gap is wider at the top than the bottom – or vice-versa – check the hinges to see whether one or other is loose or worn.

You may be able to make sufficient adjustment to reduce the gap by packing out one or other of the hinge leaves. To do this, remove the hinge leaf from the door frame and fix a thin piece of card or wood the same size as the recess, gluing and pinning it in position, before fitting back the hinge leaf.

If you find there is a wide gap down the whole edge of the door, you should be able to reduce this by gluing and pinning a thin strip of wood the same width as that of the door to the closing edge of the door to fill the gap. When doing this, you will have to remove and replace the lock's striker plate. Make sure you leave a gap of 3 mm ($\frac{1}{8}$ in) between the door and the frame when the door is closed. Rub down the new strip of wood with medium glasspaper, after filling any cracks and joins with a suitable filler, then apply primer, undercoat and a coat of gloss paint to match the existing colour scheme.

If you have tackled the problem using one of these methods, but have failed to eliminate the gap completely, you should fit an atomic type of insulating strip which will spring against the edge of the door to effect a complete seal (see page 84). You can use the rubber type of strip. If you do, however, you must make sure that the door will shut properly after it is fitted. In this case you may need to adjust the striker plate.

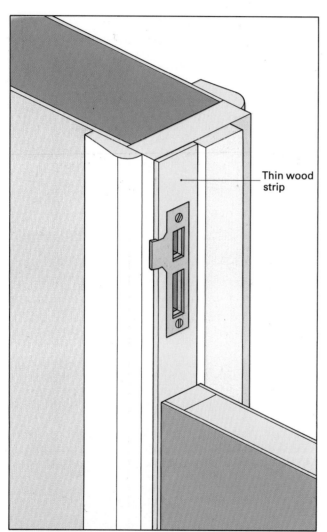

Thin wood strip

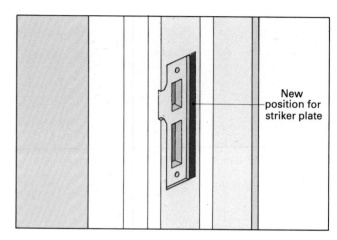

New position for striker plate

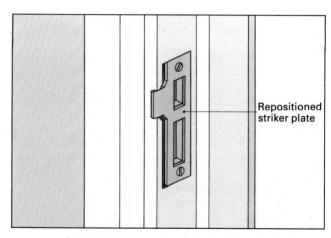

Repositioned striker plate

If you have a poorly fitting door through which draughts are finding their way, you may be able to cure this by adjusting the position of the lock's striker plate. With the door closed and on the latch, push it back and measure the slack between the door and the closing frame. Mark out the required new position of the striker plate, chisel out the necessary wood to refit the plate, screw it in position and fill the old gaps.

As already mentioned, the gap at the top of the door is not normally so critical. If you need to close the gap here for any reason, then you can use the method of fixing a strip of wood along the edge of the door as described above. You can fit insulation strip here as well.

You may find in some cases that the gap at the top is uneven because rising-butt hinges have been fitted and the door frame has been incorrectly shaped to enable the door to be opened (see below).

The most uncomfortable draughts will normally be through the bottom of the door and there are several ways of overcoming this problem. If the room into which the door opens has carpet on the floor, then there must be sufficient clearance for the door to be opened without rubbing over the carpet. Equally, the bottom of the door should rest just a fraction above the carpet and not well clear of it.

The traditional way of achieving this is to fit rising-butt hinges to the door. These enable the door to be lifted clear of the carpet as it is opened and will normally give the door a self-closing action when you shut it.

Fitting rising-butt hinges When buying these hinges, make sure you get them to open (or rise) the correct way – either left-hand or right-hand, depending on which side of the door the existing hinges are fixed and whether the door opens inwards or outwards. Remove the door by releasing the hinge leaves attached to its edge and then take out the hinges from the door frame. Check that the bottom of the door is smooth and round off the corners slightly with medium glasspaper to prevent wear on the carpet near the threshold as the door closes. Stand the door in position with the bottom edge resting on the carpet and mark the hinge positions on the door and the door frame. These should be roughly 150–200 mm (6–8 in) from the top and 175–225 mm (7–9 in) from the bottom of the door and frame.

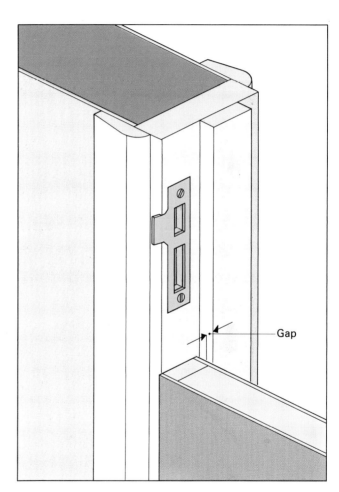

If you have a large gap on the locking edge of the door, you can reduce this by fitting a thin strip of wood inside the door frame. You must remove and remount the striker plate. Remember to leave clearance for the door to close.

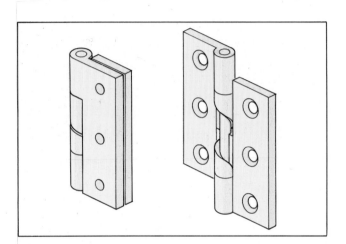

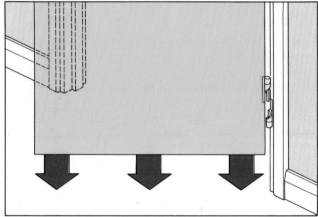

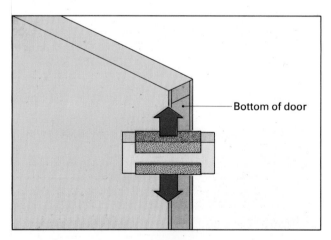

Bottom of door

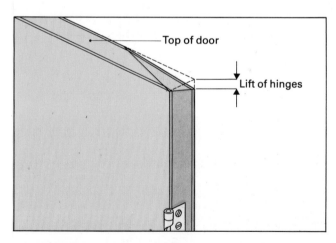

Top of door

Lift of hinges

There are two types of rising-butt hinge – for left and right-hand opening doors. Check you buy the right type. Before fitting the hinges, remove the sharp edges from both bottom corners of the door with medium glasspaper.

Fit the hinges with just one screw each and check that the door just rests on the carpet. Then try closing the door gently and plane off just enough from the top corner to allow the door to close snugly.

You will probably be able to make use of the existing hinge recesses, but minor adjustments will almost certainly have to be made. The height will probably have to be increased slightly to make sure the door just touches the carpet. Usually the leaves of rising-butt hinges are thicker than normal ones, which will involve making the recesses slightly deeper. You can do this by carefully chiselling out a bit more wood from the edge of the door and the frame.

Make sure you shape the top corner of the door on the hinge side (see diagram on page 90) to enable the door to open out from the frame without catching.

Fit the hinges to the door frame first using just one screw for each leaf, then to the door. The pin fixing is fitted to the frame. Carefully lower the door into position and then open and close it to check for the correct action. If it opens and shuts smoothly, you can then fit the rest of the screws through the hinge leaves.

If you find the door is too high or too low, make the necessary adjustments to the position of the hinges, then fix the hinge leaves back using a different screw hole. When you have achieved the correct position, you can fit the remaining screws in place.

Another way of reducing the gap at the bottom of the door is to fit a thin length of batten – probably about 4 mm (or $\frac{3}{16}$ in) underneath the carpet across the threshold. You can screw this into position, bearing in mind that if you have a solid floor you will first have to drill and plug fixing holes in the concrete. This will raise the carpet under the door when it is shut to provide the necessary seal.

Fitting draught excluders If you decide to fit a draught excluder to the bottom edge of the door to seal the gap, it is important that this does not rub heavily over the carpet as the door is opened. If it does, it will cause undue wear on that section of carpet.

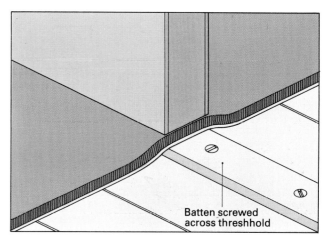

Batten screwed across threshhold

This method is only suitable to close up a very small gap at the bottom of a door, using a thin strip of batten fixed under the carpet. If the gap is more than 4 mm (or 3/16 in), you should fit a proprietary draught excluder.

There are several types of draught excluder that fit to the bottom of the door or across the threshold – or both. The more efficient fittings incorporate an aluminium frame with an inverted U-shaped vinyl insert that presses against the bottom of the door when closed. With this type it helps if you shape the bottom edge to a taper (see picture on page 92).

Apart from a vinyl strip seal, excluders are also available with a continuous brush-type seal. These are particularly suitable where there is no threshold in the doorway and where the flooring is of parquet, sheet vinyl or tiles.

The various types of draught excluder involve different methods of fixing (see pictures on page 92).

Filling holes Do not forget to check around the outside edge of the door frame where it meets the wall. Quite frequently you will get draughts through the architrave or moulding around the frame. You

A selection of proprietary draught excluders that can be fitted to the bottom of a door to eliminate draughts in this area – (from left) aluminium and vinyl flip-flop, aluminium and brush and two styles of plastic brush. There is a wide range on the market, but make sure the one you buy is suitable for the floor covering.

These examples show how you should fit either a flip-flop or brush-type draught excluder to the bottom of an internal door. These are suitable with hard floor coverings such as wood, cork or vinyl. Measure carefully where on the bottom of the door to screw in the aluminium or plastic strip so that the bottom edge of the excluder just touches the floor. Where a threshold is fitted, fix the excluder to the opposite side of the door.

These inverted 'U' type draught excluders vary from the other types in that they are fixed to the floor and the door presses on to them when closed.

When you fit the inverted 'U' type draught excluders, the bottom edge of the door should be planed to a slight taper to provide the best effect. These excluders can be fitted whether or not there is a threshold across the door.

can repair any cracks or gaps here using a suitable interior filler. Also check that there are no draughts coming from between the threshold and the floor. If there are, seal any gaps with a non-setting mastic.

Curing draughts through external doors

The problems you are likely to come across with draughty doors will be much greater with external than internal doors, particularly on windy days. The normal range of insulation strip will probably not be robust enough or suitable in these conditions.

The first thing to check is that the door closes properly without sticking to any part of the frame. Where this has happened, it is due to the door or frame – or both – swelling or warping where it has got damp and then dried out. This, of course, is not a problem with the modern aluminium or PVC doors and frames, which are not affected by damp conditions. They may also have some means of adjustment in the event of a poor fit, but you should check on this with the manufacturer's instructions.

With wooden doors and frames, the best time to test the fit is after a prolonged wet spell when any swelling will be most evident. The easiest way to locate where the door may be catching or sticking to the frame is by rubbing chalk all round the closing edge of the frame. Where this chalk is deposited on the door when shut will indicate the areas that need to be planed down.

Using a smoothing plane or chisel, ease off these parts of the closing edge of the door, rub the surface smooth with medium glasspaper and then paint over with primer, undercoat and topcoat to match the existing paintwork.

If, after planing down the edges, you still find that the door is sticking or catching, check that there

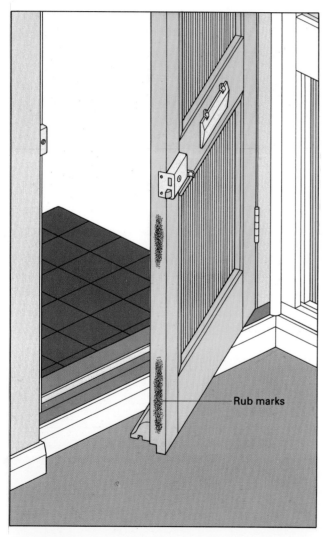

Rub marks

Poorly fitting doors will invite draughts. To check where a door may be sticking, rub chalk round the closing edges of the frame and shut the door. Plane down those areas where there are chalk deposits.

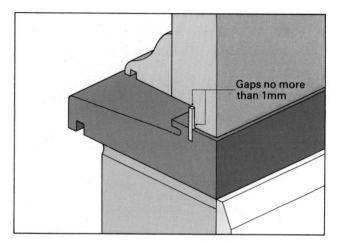

Gaps no more than 1mm

The weatherstrip across the sill prevents draughts from blowing through under the door. There will be a very small gap around it to enable the door to open and close easily and this you can ignore.

is a slight clearance between the bottom edge of the door and the weatherstrip. This is a metal strip that projects slightly from the floor across the threshold. If the door is catching on this weatherstrip, have a look at the hinges to make sure they are securely fitted and not worn. Adjust or replace them if necessary.

If the hinges are sound, then open the door and hammer down the weatherstrip using a block of wood as padding. Sometimes the dampness around the threshold can cause the weatherstrip to rise in its retaining slot. Should this fail to cure the problem, you can file down the top edge of the weatherstrip where it catches the door until it clears the bottom edge.

Close the door and check that the latch and lock function properly and hold the closing face of the door flush with the closing edge of the frame. If there is a gap here, you can adjust the position of the latch

The three basic types of threshold draught excluders shown above are all for external doors. They are made from aluminium with either vinyl or rubber seals.
The draught excluder shown top right is for an inward opening external door. The lower threshold strip should press tightly against the door when it is closed. If the door opens outwards, fit the weatherstrip against the other side of the door.
The draught excluder shown centre right is for an inward opening exterior door. It should be fitted in place with sealing compound or cement. This type cannot be used with an outward opening door.
The draught excluder shown below right is suitable with an inward and outward opening external door. The smaller weathertrim is more suited to sheltered locations.

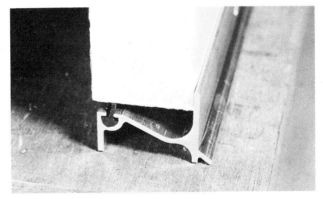

This brush type excluder, which is easily screwed to the door, protects that often forgotten area – the letterbox.

and striker plate to take up the clearance as you would for an internal door.

With the door now closing properly, check round the outside of the frame, both from the inside and outside of the house. Where the door has been slammed or forced shut, you may find the frame has worked loose and gaps will have appeared between it and the wall. You can fill these from the outside with a little concrete or a suitable exterior plaster filler and from the inside with more plaster filler or mastic. Ram the filler firmly into the gap to seal it completely, hold the frame securely and prevent any draughts getting through.

Do not forget to check below the door sill in case the mortar has crumbled away. If there is a gap, you can fill it with a mix of three parts sand to one part cement or a setting-type mastic. Remember that this filling may have to take the weight of people coming through the door.

Another part of the door to check is where the closing face at the bottom meets the weatherstrip, since often there is a small gap here.

The easiest way to measure any clearance is to stick two or three small balls of plasticine to the face of the weatherstrip that comes into contact with the door. Cover the pieces of plasticine with a single thickness of newspaper and close the door on to them. When you open the door again these balls will have been squashed down to the thickness of the gap. If this gap is more than a millimetre, you can seal it using a suitable type of insulation strip stuck to the closing face on the bottom of the door.

If there is no weatherstrip fitted across the threshold and you do not have a weatherboard fixed across the bottom of the outside of the door to take the rain that runs down the door clear of the threshold, then you can use one of the many kits available to protect this area.

The simplest comprises of an aluminium weather trim that you can screw on to the bottom of the door.

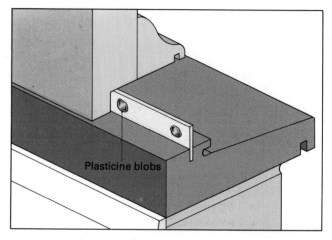

If you place plasticine along the closing face of the weatherstrip and shut the door, you can measure any gap. If this is more than 1 mm, you should fit insulation strip.

It also has a matching aluminium sill with a built-in weatherstrip and vinyl seal which you screw down on to your existing threshold. There is a more complicated version, made from galvanised steel and set in PVC, to give complete protection for those doors on a particularly exposed side of the house.

When you fit one of these kits, make sure you fix it in place over a layer of non-setting mastic to ensure that you seal off any possible gaps under the trim. This will prevent water or draughts finding their way through.

Curing draughts round skirting boards and flooring

The older the house, the more chance there is that any wooden floor may have dropped and opened up a slight gap under the skirting boards. If you have a fitted carpet in the room, you are unlikely to be troubled by this gap, since the pile of the carpet will act as a seal. You will, however, have to seal off any gaps if the floor has a hard covering such as parquet, vinyl or rigid tiles.

The best way to fill this gap is to remove the skirting boards and lower them to the new level of the floor.

If you do not want to go to the trouble of resiting all the skirting boards round the room, you can fill any gaps with a suitable interior mastic filler, which you should pack well into the holes. With larger gaps it is a good idea to stuff these with paper first then finish off with filler. This means that you do not use too much filler and do not waste it by letting it fall through the gap.

You will sometimes find in older houses that the floorboards are plain-edged and not tongued and grooved. Equally, if tongued and grooved boards

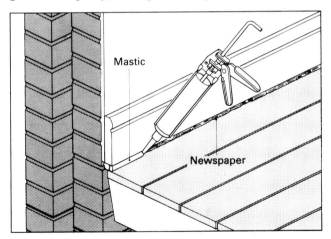

To fill gaps between the skirting board and the floor, use non-setting mastic in a colour to suit the decoration. Where these gaps are large, stuff newspaper into the holes before applying the mastic on top.

have had to be lifted for any reason, such as to gain access to electrical circuits or plumbing pipes, the tongue will have been sawn through. In either case, any draughts under the floor will find their way through.

The most satisfactory way of eliminating this problem is by laying carpet or a similar type of overall covering such as sheet vinyl on the floor. You can also fill individual gaps or cracks with wood filler or a non-setting mastic.

Checking draughts through chimneys

As has already been discussed, chimneys provide the most convenient exit for warm air in a room and this results in cold air being drawn into the room to replace it. It is therefore obvious that any steps that can be taken to reduce the flow of air up a chimney that does not constitute a safety hazard – by affecting the necessary escape of fumes – will help reduce the problem of draughts.

If an existing chimney is no longer being used for a solid, liquid or gas-fuelled fire appliance, you can cap it. But you must still provide some ventilation in the chimney to prevent possible trouble from condensation or damp inside, which could eventually affect the walls against the chimney.

The first job is to have the chimney cleaned thoroughly to remove any deposits of soot and debris that could otherwise fall to the bottom and cause smells. You can block off the fire opening with a sheet of hardboard or plasterboard, for example. If you do, make sure you cut a small horizontal slit – about 75 × 12 mm (3 × ½ in) – in the board near floor level to provide adequate ventilation. It is best to remove the fireplace completely so that you can block off the opening down to the floor and replaster the new panel and joins with the surrounding wall to

Before attempting to remove an unwanted fireplace, always sweep the chimney clean. The surround can be eased away from the wall with crowbars. Use packing behind them to save damaging the plaster. Hold the

surround to prevent it falling forwards. When you have removed it from the wall, clear away any loose plaster. You should be able to lift away the plinth with crowbars as well. If it is made of concrete, chip this away.

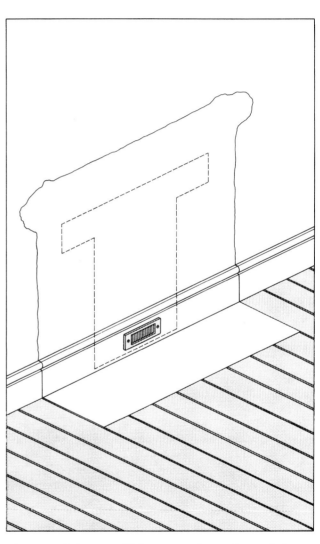

Having removed the fireplace surround, line the opening with a suitable sized sheet of hardboard. Remember to cut out a small ventilation hole at the bottom. Depending on how badly damaged the surrounding plasterwork is, you will have to make good round the edges of the hardboard with extra plaster before decorating. If fitting skirting board at the bottom, cut a hole and mount the ventilation grille over it.

provide a neat, flush finish before redecorating.

Removing a fireplace This is not too difficult a job to carry out yourself, although it can be messy and you should take the precaution of laying dust sheets over the area around the fireplace.

Most tiled surrounds are fixed to the wall with nails or screws. To remove the wall-mounted part of the fireplace, drive in a small crowbar or similar tool at each side towards the top and then lever the surround away from the wall. If necessary you can cut off any exposed nails or screws with a hacksaw. This will enable you to lift the complete surround away from the wall and remove it. If it proves cumbersome, you can break it up into smaller sections using a club hammer. Make sure if you do this that you are wearing protective goggles to stop any flying pieces going in your eyes.

Having removed the fireplace surround, you should then be able to lift up the hearth.

You will be left with a rectangular hole in the wall. The easiest way to cover this up is with a suitable size piece of hardboard or plasterboard (see diagram). You can fix this in place using masonry nails or 32 mm ($1\frac{1}{4}$ in) No 8 countersunk screws at 150 mm (or 6 in) intervals around the edges of the board. Do not forget to cut out a small ventilation slit as mentioned above.

To finish off the job, you will have to repair the damaged edges of the wall with a suitable bonding plaster. Then redecorate over the new board to match the existing decor in the room.

The floor under the hearth will normally be intact. If not, you may have to use some self-levelling screeding compound to ensure a neat finish here too.

If you are not using the chimney again, you can blank off the top with a metal or porcelain capping cowl. Alternatively you can insert an airbrick into the top course of bricks in the chimney stack and seal off the opening with concrete flaunching, using a tile or slate to cover up the hole.

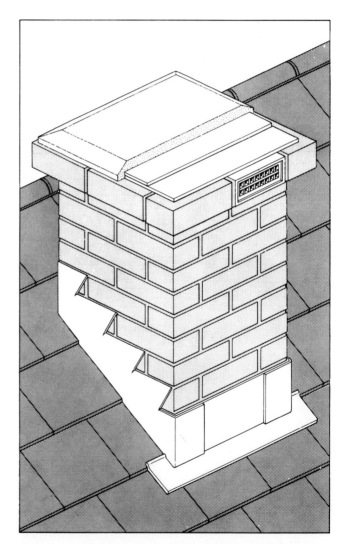

When you cap the chimney, do not forget to incorporate an airbrick or similar means of ventilation around the top. To prevent excessive down-draughts, this should face away from the prevailing wind.

6 Double glazing

It used to be claimed that double glazing was the most beneficial and effective means of insulating the home. With the rise in prices and more accurate costings on other forms of home insulation, it is now recognised that it can take a considerable time – in most cases between 6 and 12 years – for double glazing to pay for itself in terms of savings in fuel.

There are, however, other benefits to be gained from fitting double glazing which need to be taken into consideration and may help to justify the high initial outlay on this type of insulation. Correctly fitted double glazing will cut out draughts through windows and glass doors, give extra security and help reduce noise levels outside. It will also allow more 'living' space inside, since you will be able to sit much closer to a double-glazed window without any of the discomfort you might have suffered from a single-glazed one.

Most of the modern replacement window systems that include double glazing are in aluminium or uPVC and do not require painting, thus bringing a considerable saving in maintenance costs. Whenever windows need to be replaced, you are advised to use double-glazed ones.

Although it is difficult to put an exact value on these added advantages, they obviously contribute to the value of a double glazing system and do help to make it a worthwhile investment in the long term.

The value of double glazing

In the average house, windows are the worst areas for insulation. To take an example, the typical U value for a single-glazed metal-framed window is 5.6 and for a single-glazed wooden-framed window 4.3. With such high U values, it is obvious that a considerable amount of heat is lost through the windows of the home. How much will depend on the size of each window, but on average 10–20% of your valuable heat will disappear this way.

Of course heat loss is not the only problem with single-glazed windows. These are a notorious source of draughts, as well as providing the 'false draught' effect caused by the cold internal surface of the glass. Double glazing will cope with all these problems.

The principle of double glazing is a relatively simple one. Instead of a single pane of glass in the window, a second pane is fitted inside it and the gap between them sealed so that the trapped air acts as an insulator. This reduces the U value considerably – and the wider the gap, the lower the U value. With a 6 mm ($\frac{1}{4}$ in) air gap, for example, the U value is 3.4, with a 12 mm ($\frac{1}{2}$ in) gap 3.0 and a 20 mm (or $\frac{1}{4}$ in) gap 2.9.

The most widely used form of double glazing makes use of hermetically sealed double glazing units. These are most frequently fitted in replacement windows, although it is sometimes possible to fit sealed units to an existing frame. The great advantage of sealed unit double glazing over secondary sash double glazing is that you have all the benefits of double glazing but still only two faces of the glass to keep clean.

When double glazing is installed in replacement windows, because the windows are new and to modern design standards, they will also take care of eliminating the draughts because they are made with this in mind. The air gaps between the panes of double glazing in a sealed unit vary from 6 mm ($\frac{1}{4}$ in) to 20 mm ($\frac{3}{4}$ in), with the highest insulation being achieved with the 20 mm ($\frac{3}{4}$ in) gap.

Another method of double glazing involves fitting secondary windows on the inside of the whole window frame. These can be sliding, hinged or detachable to enable you to open them easily for cleaning – or when you want to let in air through the

Double glazing is available for all types of windows and glass doors – including patio doors. The products on the market include a whole range of finishes to suit individual locations. Since the initial outlay can be considerable, you should choose carefully the type that best suits your situation and requirements. Your choice includes complete replacement sections or secondary frames which fit inside existing frames.

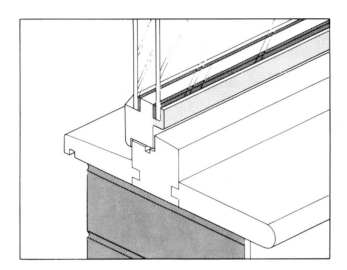

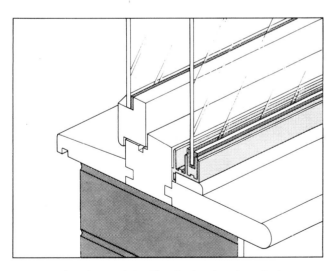

The simplest form of double glazing involves fitting an additional frame on to the existing opening frame (top). More effective is the secondary frame (above) – hinged or sliding – which cuts out draughts round the frame.

outer windows during warm weather.

Secondary sash double glazing is usually cheaper to fit than replacement windows and can be used to provide wider air gaps between the panes than with sealed units. This can be an advantage where noise insulation is a particularly severe problem.

All double glazing provides insulation against the entry of unwanted noise. Where this is particularly severe, however, air gaps of up to 200 mm (or 8 in) are recommended. At that figure, you will achieve the maximum effective level of noise insulation.

Double glazing will normally reduce condensation and prevent damage to wooden window sills caused by the moisture running down the glass on to them. This is because with double glazing the inside surface of the glass is not as cold as with a single pane. However it can also make the problem of condensation worse, since it stops those draughts needed to ensure adequate ventilation in the room. To overcome this problem, some alternative form of ventilation must be found for the room.

Safety One important point you should bear in mind is that in the event of a fire windows are quite often the only means of escape from a room. It is therefore always desirable to have at least one window in a room that is capable of being opened wide enough to serve as an emergency escape exit.

Even more important, however, you should ensure that all glazing conforms at least to the minimum safety standards laid down in BS 6262. There are 20,000 domestic accidents a year in the UK involving windows and nearly all these could be avoided if the right glazing is selected in the first place.

Using the professional

With more and more emphasis being put on home insulation and conservation of energy, the double glazing market has been enjoying a boom period. In such a situation there is ample opportunity for inexperienced and ill-equipped companies and fitters to ply their 'trade'. Obvious targets are large housing estates, where a never-ending stream of glossy literature pours through the letterboxes.

Unfortunately the image of the double glazing salesman has not survived without criticism, although the majority of the major companies selling this type of insulation have established and do maintain a reputation for reliability and fair practice. Equally there are many local contractors on whom you can rely to supply quality material and fit it correctly.

The Glass and Glazing Federation has a code of ethical practice, drawn up in conjuction with the Office of Fair Trading, covering the whole area of double glazing – or indeed any glazing – for purchase by consumers for installation in their home.

The following recommendations are designed to help you make the best choice if you decide to have double glazing professionally installed. Most companies offer either complete replacement windows or secondary windows to fit inside your existing frames. Replacement windows are more expensive than secondary ones, so you should consider the various benefits of each type of double glazing before making your decision.

Inspect the existing frames yourself to check on their condition. Use a small screwdriver for this, testing all areas of woodwork, especially around the bottom of the frames. If the blade goes in easily, then the wood is rotten and you will need to replace the window anyway. Surface damage can be repaired if the majority of the frame is still sound. Equally sills can be replaced, if these are badly damaged or rotten, without changing the whole window.

The range of replacement windows is large and varied. If you do decide you need this work done, you should insist on a hardwood surround for the window. Most windows are now 'maintenance free', which means they are made of aluminium, stove-

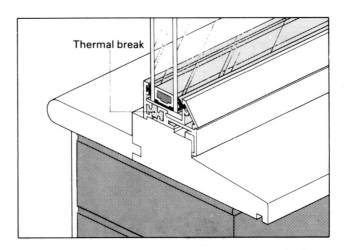

The use of a plastic thermal barrier in double-glazed frames reduces the conduction of cold temperatures onto the inside frame – and therefore condensation.

enamelled or plastic-coated aluminium or white uPVC.

One aspect of aluminium windows you should check on is whether they incorporate a thermal barrier. This means that the outside aluminium frame is not in metal-to-metal contact with the inside frame but separated, normally with a plastic joint. The effect of this barrier is to reduce the conduction of cold outside temperatures into the inside frame.

Without this thermal barrier the cold frame is quickly covered with condensation, which then runs down the frame to the inside sill where it can cause a lot of damage if left unchecked.

Fitting your own

There are many different types of double glazing available should you decide to fit it yourself and many factors to consider in making your choice.

These include the type of window you are working with, the cost and ease of installation and how effective you want the double glazing to be.

Glass or plastic? Some of the larger double glazing companies use a special type of glass in their windows which has been treated on one side to allow the heat from the sun to pass through into the room but resist the passage of heat from the room to the outside. This type of glass does not deteriorate as it gets older, is difficult to scratch and will maintain its one-way heat conducting properties. It is called low emissivity glass and is now readily available on the domestic market.

The thickness of glass you need will vary. But unless you are fitting your double glazing to very small or very large panes, you will normally need glass that is 4–6 mm (or $\frac{1}{8}$–$\frac{1}{4}$ in) thick. Always check with your glass supplier or the manufacturer of the fittings you are using on the recommended thickness of glass to suit individual situations and that it complies with the minimum safety standard laid down in BS 6262.

In addition to the normal float glass, there are several other types of glass that are more resistant to breakages. These are especially recommended for patio doors and full-length windows, since they are shatterproof and will withstand anyone accidentally walking into them or knocking something against them. You must, however, check on the safety aspect in the event of a fire, should you want to fit stronger glass into ordinary windows. The more common types available are toughened and laminated glass. On impact, these will either remain unbroken or break safely – as defined in BS 6206.

The choice of plastics is also extensive and it is not always easy to decide on their relative merits. All plastic sheet has less clarity than glass and this is gradually worsened due to the effects of ultra-violet rays when exposed to sunlight. If you fit plastic panes inside glass ones, the amount of light passing into the room is considerably reduced. It is, however, advisable to remove plastic panes during the summer and store them in a cool, dark spot to prolong their life.

Acrylic is the best type of plastic for clarity and if it is fitted carefully and removed during the summer it should last intact for 10 years or more. Clear polystyrene used in a similar way will probably last from six to eight years.

All types of plastic sheet are prone to scratchmarks and you should be particularly careful when it comes to cleaning them. Make sure you only use a non-abrasive, non-scratch cleaner. When you clean plastic, static electricity is generated which tends to attract dust. The plastic will soon become coated with dust unless you use a special anti-static polish. Check, therefore, that the polish you use is suitable for the type of plastic you fit and ensure that it does not contain any harmful solvents that might damage the surface.

When you buy plastic sheets, they may be protected by a paper or film covering. Keep this on while storing and until after you have cut the sheets to size to maintain the protection prior to fitting.

You must also check that where plastics are used for glazing they comply with the minimum safety standards laid down in BS 6262, especially where low-level glazing, door or door side panels are concerned. Where that standard requires safety glazing materials that comply with BS 6206 Type A, B or C, plastic materials are available which meet this requirement. It is very important that you check this out at the time of purchase.

The following list of the more common plastics includes the normal thicknesses available and some individual characteristics (all plastics can be cut to size quite easily (see below); you may have to buy full sheets of standard sizes and then cut them to suit your requirements). The types are listed in order of cost, with the cheapest first.

Clear PVC film This is not really clear enough for general double glazing, but you could use it in bedrooms and other areas where you do not normally look out through the windows during the day. It is supplied from the roll 0.25 and 0.5 mm (0.01 and 0.02 in) thick. It will need to be supported on a frame to keep it rigid and will probably only last a year or so, after which time you can replace the film.

Clear polyester film This is clearer, stronger yet thinner than clear PVC and can be used in similar circumstances. It is also available from the roll 0.125 and 0.175 mm (0.005 and 0.007 in) thick.

Clear polystyrene sheet This rigid sheet plastic is affected by ultra-violet rays, retains a static charge and will burn easily. It is claimed to have a life of between six and eight years if stored in a cool, dark place during the summer. The sheets are supplied in 2, 3 or 4 m ($\frac{1}{16}$, $\frac{1}{8}$ or $\frac{3}{16}$ in) thicknesses.

Clear acrylic sheet This type of plastic is available in extruded or cast sheets. The extruded sheets are not really suitable for double glazing since they contain defects leading to distortion and warping. Acrylic is claimed to have an impact strength 12 times that of glass, has better optical properties than polystyrene and has an anticipated life of 10 years or more. It does, however, burn easily. Any scratches in it can be cleaned out with a metal polish, but you will need special anti-static polish to avoid an accumulation of dust. The cast sheets are available in 3, 4 or 6 mm ($\frac{1}{8}$, $\frac{3}{16}$ or $\frac{1}{4}$ in) thicknesses. High impact acrylic, with a claimed strength 60 times that of glass, is also available in 3 mm ($\frac{1}{8}$ in) thickness.

Clear rigid PVC sheet This has a high-impact strength, stronger than wired glass. It is not quite as clear as acrylic, but has a guaranteed minimum life of 10 years. One advantage is that it has a self-extinguishing fire rating that conforms to building regulations for roofs. This type of plastic sheet is available in 3 mm ($\frac{1}{8}$ in) thickness.

Clear polycarbonate sheet This has a claimed impact strength 800 times that of glass. It is ultra-violet stabilised for long life and is self-extinguishing in the event of fire. It comes in 3, 4 or 6 mm ($\frac{1}{8}$, $\frac{3}{16}$ or $\frac{1}{4}$ in) thicknesses.

Although plastic has a lower thermal conductivity than glass, there is not a significant difference in the relative U values. The high impact-resistance offered by some plastics is an important security factor and may well be considered an advantage in areas of potential danger, such as in a child's bedroom, provided that the windows can be opened from the inside in the event of an emergency.

Plastic is, of course, easier to cut and fit than glass and safe to handle. It is normally thinner than glass, but the thickness you would need will almost certainly be governed by the range of fittings you are using. With the exception of film, plastic sheeting is normally more expensive than glass.

The life of all plastics is limited, depending on the type you choose, and all are easily scratched and will carry a static charge. From the safety point of view, cheaper plastics are not fire-resistant and all can be affected by such things as cigarette burns.

Types of fittings

Many different systems are available if you decide to fit your own double glazing. Most take the form of secondary windows fitted to the surrounding frame of the whole window, while others enable additional panes to be fitted to any individual frame, whether opening or fixed. To fit a secondary window to a surrounding frame, this frame needs to be at least 20 mm ($\frac{3}{4}$ in) wide to enable you to secure the glazing bars that hold the glass or rigid plastic. If not, you will have to fit the double glazing on to the window reveal or the surrounding internal brickwork using a

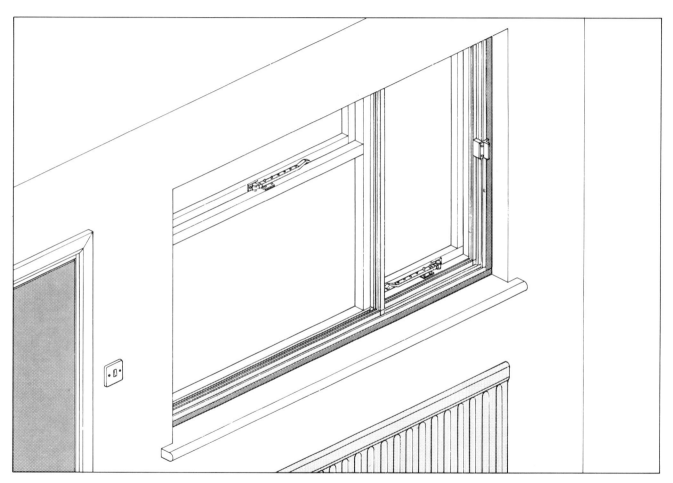

timber mounting frame at least 25 mm (1 in) thick all round the reveal.

The various double glazing alternatives described below are all for fitting additional panes over existing ones. Before you decide where to site the secondary glazing, bear in mind that the larger the air gap between that and the existing window the lower the U value and the greater the insulation properties,

When fitting secondary double glazing, you mount the new frame directly on to the window reveal, if it is square. Although it involves slightly more preparatory work, you will find it a lot easier if you fit a timber framework with battens inside the reveal and mount the secondary glazing to this. Not only can you ensure the framework is square, but it is also much easier to fix the systems to wood than to brickwork.

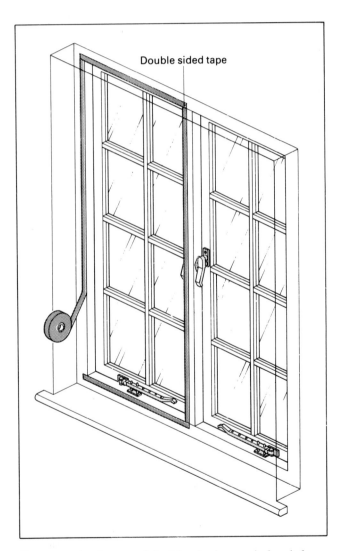

Double sided tape

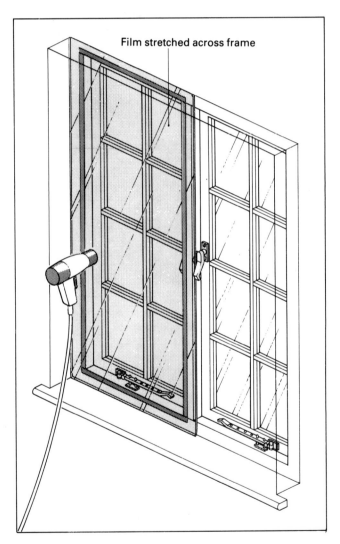

Film stretched across frame

One very simple way of double-glazing a window is by fixing thermal seal film over the panes with double-sided tape. Stick the tape all round the opening frame, then stretch the film as tightly as you can on to it, allowing a slight overlap. By playing a hair dryer over the film, you will shrink the film taut and remove any creases. Finally trim off the overlap with scissors or a knife. This system will only last for a season.

both of heat and sound. You should not, however, install the glazing with an air gap of more than 200 mm (or 8 in), since the air inside any larger cavity can circulate and reduce the effect of the insulation.

To function properly, the air gap between the panes must be sealed, otherwise you will get condensation between the panes. This means that when you initially seal off the gap, the inside surfaces of both panes must be spotlessly clean and the air inside dry. To ensure this, never seal off the panes when the room is full of hot, damp air. Use a silicone cleaner on the insides of the panes.

Curtains Whether or not you install a double glazing system, heavy curtains can, when drawn across the window, drastically reduce loss of heat from the room. You can make this more efficient by sealing the outside edges of the curtains to the walls with double-sided adhesive tape. Make sure that your curtains do not hang over any radiator that is positioned under a window. If they do, the heat rising from them will be guided up into and through the window and not into the room.

Using thermal seal film This is similar to cling film, but more efficient and better to look at. First stick the special double-sided adhesive tape recommended all round the window frame to be treated. Then stretch the film as tightly as possible over the frame, sticking the edges down on to the tape with a 50 mm (2 in) overlap. When the film is stuck down, play a hair dryer over it. This will cause it to shrink and tighten and remove any creases, giving a clear, flat second pane. Finally trim off the overlapping film with a pair of scissors. At the end of the winter, you can remove the film and tape and replace them in the autumn.

Using a touch-and-close film system This type of system is designed for use with PVC and polyester films. The fastener resembles Velcro strip and incorporates lengths of hookside and loopside tape.

To fit the touch-and-close system, measure and cut the hookside tape and fit it round the plastic film. Fix correct lengths of loopside tape on to the hookside tape, then position the film on the frame. To remove it, simply peel back the film.

Clean the window and frame and dry them thoroughly. Then cut a piece of film – the correct size – measured to the outside edges of the fastener tape. Measure and cut four lengths of hookside tape to correspond to the top, bottom and sides of the film and stick these carefully on to the edges of one side of the film. Next position the loopside of the tape on to the hookside and remove the backing on the top edge of the film. Position the piece of film correctly over the window and press the top strip of fastener so that you have a sound contact with the frame along its width. Remove the backing from the three remaining strips and carefully press the two sides and bottom into place. Make sure there are no creases in the film as you do this.

This system is only intended to last one year. Although the touch-and-close fastener may be used for rigid plastic panes, the method does not give a particularly pleasing appearance.

Using a magnetic strip system   This is based on the fastener system just described, but uses a magnetic strip which is stuck to the plastic pane and a metal strip which is fitted to the window frame. It is intended for use with 2–4 mm ($\frac{1}{16}$–$\frac{3}{16}$ in) acrylic sheet and has the advantage that the fixing does not show when you remove the pane in the summer.

Make sure you cut the plastic pane to overlap each edge of the frame by about 12 mm ($\frac{1}{2}$ in). Hold the pane in position over the frame and draw around it with a pencil. Remove the backing from the metal strip and stick this on to the frame against this marked line. You can give this strip just one coat of paint to match the colour of the window frame, but wait until the paint is dry before you fit the pane in place. Then stick the magnetic strip carefully in position on the back of the pane – one length top and bottom and one length on either side.

When you place the pane on the frame it will automatically fix itself on to the metal strip. With larger panes you should also fit two glazing clips

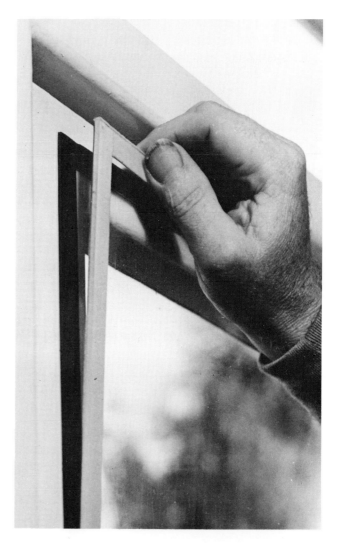

To fit the magnetic strip system, mark the position of the plastic pane on the opening frame and stick on the metal strip. Fix the magnetic strip round the edges of the pane and then position this over the metal strip.

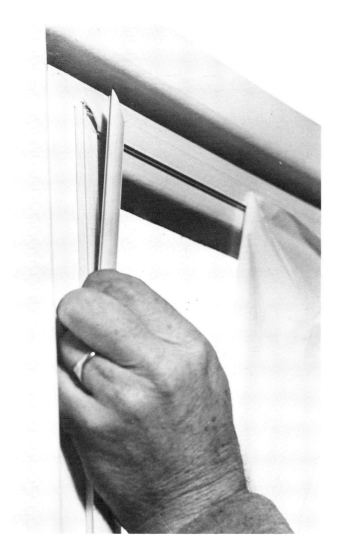

When fitting the PVC channel and retainer system, mitre each corner of the self-adhesive channel and stick it on the opening frame. Cut the plastic pane accurately to size and secure it with the outer retaining strip.

The PVC hinged system is suitable for use with opening windows and incorporates plastic panes. By fitting the window stay shown, you can hold the pane open to provide ventilation through the existing window.

along the bottom edge to provide more support and prevent the pane slipping.

Using a PVC channel and retainer system   This can be used as a fixed system on a non-opening window. Using special PVC channel with a self-adhesive foam backing – to cope with any irregularities on the window frame surface – fix the measured lengths along the top, bottom and sides of the frame, allowing approximately 20 mm ($\frac{3}{4}$ in) overlap on to the existing glass. You can mitre the corners of the PVC channel framework using the mitre block supplied with the kit.

You can use 2 or 3 mm ($\frac{1}{16}$ or $\frac{1}{8}$ in) plastic for the pane, which you fit into the frame where it is held by a special sealing edge inside. To ensure a secure fixing and a neat finish, fit measured lengths of retaining strip, which must be mitred in the same way as before, into the channel where they are held by a locking rib along each length. The pressure of the retaining strip on the panel forms an effective seal. By lifting the outside edge of the retaining strip you can easily lift out individual panes for cleaning or in case of an emergency.

Using a PVC hinged system   The hinged system is cheaper to install than a sliding one. You can either fix it over the whole window frame, if you do not need to open the window regularly, or over individual panes where these have to be opened. Although one or two systems are designed for use with plastic only, similar systems are available for use with 4 mm ($\frac{3}{16}$ in) thick glass.

You must edge each pane you are fitting with a nylon moulding. With plastic you just stick the moulding on to the four edges with the adhesive supplied. Glass sheets are held in place by tight-fitting, soft plastic seals along the edges.

The special moulding incorporates a double-winged seal around the edge which closes against the frame. Three of the edges have plain mouldings fitted, while the fourth has a plastic hinge along its

length to allow the pane to be opened for cleaning.
Using sliding and hinged double glazing   These systems, which are very popular, use glass panes held in PVC or aluminium frames. The method of fitting these types of secondary glazing is explained in the picture sequences.

With the sliding version, you can move the panes either horizontally or vertically. The principle of installation involves making up an outer framework, which is fixed either to the existing window frame or to the reveal. Each pane is fitted with a rigid frame made up of channel sections screwed or clipped together at the corners. These frames slide in the runners of the outer framework and a seal is fitted to all closing edges to prevent draughts.

The hinged version also uses glass and the panes are held in similar type frames to the sliding ones. Again there is a draught seal round all edges of the frames, which are hinged on one side.

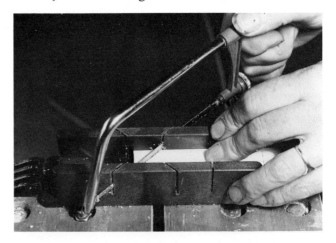

To make up the frames for a plastic hinged system, cut the frame sections to length and mitre each end, using the guide provided, with a junior hacksaw. File off the burr from the cut ends with a file for a neat finish.

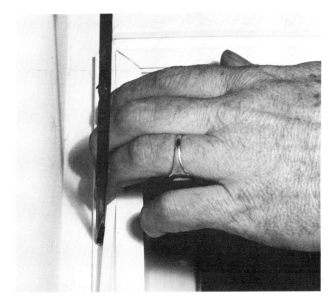

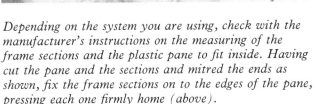

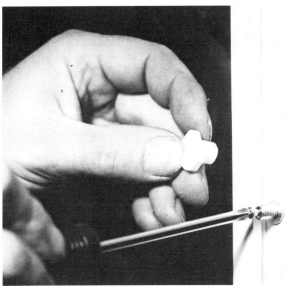

Depending on the system you are using, check with the manufacturer's instructions on the measuring of the frame sections and the plastic pane to fit inside. Having cut the pane and the sections and mitred the ends as shown, fix the frame sections on to the edges of the pane, pressing each one firmly home (above).

Offer the frame up to the existing window, making sure the hinged section is on the correct side of the existing frame for opening. Then pull back the cover strip on the hinged section to reveal the screw-fixing holes (above right). Mark through holes on to the window frame with a bradawl and then fix the hinged section of frame into place with the screws provided.

Having fitted the frame into place, locate the position for the securing buttons around the new frame according to the manufacturer's instructions and then screw these into place (right). Finally fit on the plastic caps. These hold the plastic hinged frame in position against the existing frame. To release the hinged frame you simply turn the button round.

You will find it a lot easier when fitting aluminium secondary double glazing systems to fix a timber batten framework inside the window reveal and mount the outer tracks on to it. Measure up the reveal and cut the 50 × 12 mm (2 × ½ in) batten to length. Drill fixing holes along each length, offer each batten to the reveal and mark through these holes on to the plaster. Drill and plug holes in the reveal and screw on the battens.

Before you measure up inside the timber batten framework and cut the outer aluminium tracks to length, check that the new opening is a perfect rectangle. Plane down any high spots as required. At this stage, you should fill any gaps with plaster filler and paint the framework to match the existing decoration.

First measure the distance across the top and bottom of the framework between the inside edges of the side battens. Measure and cut the top and bottom tracks to length with a hacksaw, ensuring the cut ends are square. Remove any burr with a file.

Before screwing these into place, slide the lengths of draughtproofing gasket into the channel provided inside the lengths of track, cutting off any excess gasket. These gaskets prevent draughts round the frames.

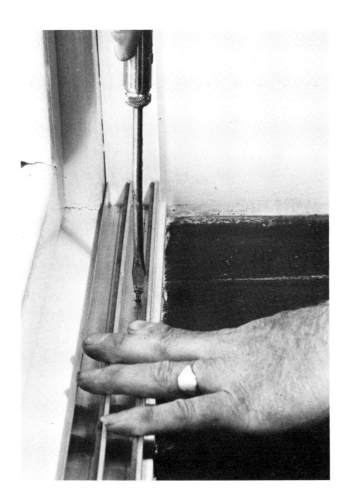
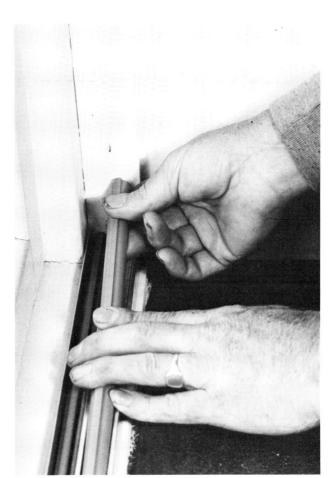

You will have to drill holes in the bottom of the track; check first with the manufacturer's instructions. Offer each length of track to the framework in turn, with the draughtproofing gaskets facing towards the existing window, and mark through the fixing holes into the timber with a bradawl. Then fix the top and bottom tracks with 12 mm ($\frac{1}{2}$ in) No 6 countersunk screws. Measure from the bottom edge of the top track to the top edge of the bottom track at each end to determine the exact length of each of the side tracks. Cut these squarely to length as before, checking that they fit tightly between the top and bottom tracks. Insert the correct length of draughtproofing gasket into each, drill fixing holes and fit each side track as for the other tracks. Then cut the plastic running track to length and fit into each of the bottom track channels.

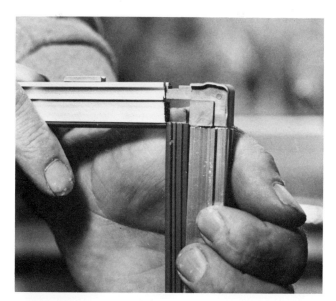

Follow the manufacturer's instructions very carefully
when measuring for the glass, making the necessary
allowances. The maximum area for a single pane is
1.8 sq m (20 sq ft). This will determine how many
panes you need to complete the window – and therefore
the number of frames to be made. Then measure up and
cut the frame sections and plastic gaskets to length and
fit these into place over the side edges of the glass,
allowing an equal gap at either end (above). Fit the
glides provided on the bottom frame section and the
handle on the correct side frame section, according to the
manufacturer's instructions. Then fit the top and bottom
sections using the corner pieces provided (above right).
Insert and tighten all the fixing screws. Cut to length
and fix the wide brush gaskets (right) to the edges of
the frames that overlap (see manufacturer's instructions)
and insert the small brush gaskets to all other edges of
the frame, holding these in place with contact adhesive
in each corner. Insert the frame into the top track, then
lower the bottom into position in the bottom track.

Useful contacts

The following should prove helpful in supplying additional information and advice on the various types of home insulation described in this book:

- The local Citizens' Advice Bureau
- The local Electricity or Gas showroom
- The local Solid Fuel Advisory Service office or Living Fire Centre (ring Sunderland 73578 for local addresses)
- The local Electricity or Gas Consumers' Council

also

- The Association of Control Manufacturers, Leicester House, 8 Leicester Street, London WC2H 2BN. Tel: 01-437 0678
- Builders Merchants Federation, 15 Soho Square, London W1. Tel: 01-439 1753
- The Cavity Foam Bureau, 9–11 The Hayes, Cardiff CF1 1NU. Tel: 0222 388621
- Draughtproofing Advisory Association Ltd, PO Box 12, Haslemere, Surrey GU27 3AN. Tel: 0428 54011
- Energy Efficiency Office, Room 1312, Thames House South, Millbank, London SW1P 4QJ. Tel: 01-211 6326
- Eurisol UK (Association of British Manufacturers of Mineral Insulating Fibres), St Paul's House, Edison Road, Bromley, Kent BR2 0EP. Tel: 01-466 6719
- External Wall Insulation Association, PO Box 12, Haslemere, Surrey GU27 3AN. Tel: 0428 54011
- Glass & Glazing Federation, 6 Mount Row, London W1Y 6DY. Tel: 01-629 8334
- Heat Pump Manufacturers Association, Nicholson House, High Street, Maidenhead, Berkshire SL6 1LF. Tel: 0628 34667/8
- The Hevac Association Automatic Controls Group, Nicholson House, High Street, Maidenhead, Berkshire SL6 1LF. Tel: 0628 34667/8
- Heating & Ventilating Contractors' Association (Home Heating Enquiry Line), 34 Palace Court, London W2 4JG. Tel: 01-229 5543
- Insulating Jacket Manufacturers' Federation, Little Burton West, Derby Street, Burton-on-Trent, Staffs DE14 1PP. Tel: 0283 63815
- Liquefied Petroleum Gas Industry Technical Association, 17 Grosvenor Crescent, London SW1X 7EJ. Tel: 01-245 9511
- National Association of Loft Insulation Contractors, PO Box 12, Haslemere, Surrey GU27 3AN. 0428 54011
- National Cavity Insulation Association, PO Box 12, Haslemere, Surrey GU27 3AN. Tel: 0428 54011
- Structural Insulation Association, 24 Ormond Road, Richmond, Surrey TW10 6TH. Tel: 01-876 4415

Index